CW00321939

THE
LADY'S DRESSING ROOM
1892

TRANSLATED FROM THE FRENCH
OF
BARONESS STAFFE

BY
LADY COLIN CAMPBELL

The woman's sanctum, care of the body,
advice and recipes,
guidance for the obese and the thin,
little hints and
twenty one pages of advertisements.

OLD HOUSE BOOKS
MORETONHAMPSTEAD DEVON

Old House Books produce facsimile copies of long out of print
books that we believe deserve a second innings. Our reprints of
detailed Victorian and Edwardian maps and guide books
are of interest to genealogists and local historians.
Other titles have been chosen to explore the character of
life in years gone by and are of interest to anyone
who wishes to know a bit more about
the lives of our forebears.

For details of other titles
published by Old House Books
please visit
www.OldHouseBooks.co.uk
or request a catalogue.

Old House Books
The Old Police Station
Pound Street
Moretonhampstead
Newton Abbot
Devon UK
TQ13 8PA

01647 440707
info@OldHouseBooks.co.uk

First published by Cassell & Company, Ltd 1892
This edition published in 2006 by
© Old House Books
ISBN-10 1 873590 62 8
ISBN-13 978 1 873590 62 1
Printed in India

CONTENTS.

PART IV.

PREFACE.

---·◆·---

Woman's Sanctum.

THERE are in every house two or three rooms on which a woman stamps her special mark, which seem to reflect her both morally and physically.

It may be her own sitting-room, where she lives her intellectual and artistic life, and where she receives her particular friends (those whom she loves and chooses above all others); it may be her bedroom, the centre of her family and conjugal affections; or it may be that holy of holies, her dressing-room, where no profane foot may enter, which is forbidden ground to her nearest and dearest—where some people imagine that she loses herself in admiration of her own perfections, like a Buddha of the

Hindoo heaven; others that she there prac-
tises all kinds of magic, in order to keep
herself so astonishingly young and lovely—
and where she assuredly does meditate how
to captivate, or to retain the heart of, the
man she loves, by cultivating the gifts that
Nature has bestowed upon her.

Whether she arms herself there for the
triumphs of vanity, or struggles for happiness by defending her beauty against the
attacks of time and the fatigues of life, it is
there that she is her real self. It may be a
luxurious room, and yet pure as the thoughts
of a young girl; it may look simple, and
yet contain the resources of diabolic
coquetry. It is here that the occupant is a
true woman, preparing for love or victory,
according to her nature; and it is here
that everything demonstrates how well she
understands the importance of the care and
attention required by the human body. It
is here that we see how by strength ot will
she can get rid of the defects with which

she has been born, or at least succeed in diminishing them.

I will not speak of women who desire to attract universal admiration, who dream of dragging at their chariot-wheels a crowd of those worthless adorers who are caught by one meaning glance; nor of such women who, led astray by a perverted desire to please, obtain their power by injurious means, and thus advance surely towards premature old age and ugliness. I will not defile the sanctum where a goddess reigns by the mention of tricks and falsehood.

I recognise only the woman anxious to preserve the love of the man of her heart, the companion of her earthly pilgrimage; the woman whose wish it is to remain attractive only to the father of her children, whose desire it is to keep the head of the house by her side, and to learn by common-sense the means of retaining for him alone the charms which have been given to her. The one who understands that healthy—I

might almost say, sacred—coquetry; whose
conscience tells her to adorn herself and to
remain beautiful, so as to be the delight
of the eyes and the joy of him who is the
support of her womanly weakness; who
requires that her mission should be to please
and to charm, to be the ideal in the rough
life of man, and to remain on the pedestal
upon which she has been placed by him
—the woman who knows these things,
and who has listened to that inward voice,
makes of her dressing-room a sanctuary
where no one, not even her husband (above
all, not her husband), may cross the thres-
hold, where she gives herself up to the
service of her beauty—a hard service at
times.   Not that she has anything to hide
that she is ashamed of, nor that she is afraid
of revealing secrets which would make her
less respected, but moved first of all by a
delicate sense of modesty, and also naturally
by a certain instinct of vanity.

How ever pretty or ideally graceful you

may be, you cannot escape a fatal absurdity at certain moments of your toilette. For instance, to take a small thing; a woman in the act of curling her hair, even if it is her own, will not appear to advantage, and may even look ridiculous. Such trivialities cause us to lose some of the halo with which we would always be surrounded in the eyes of those who love us best. Let us wrap the prosy facts of life in some little mystery; if we display them all, we shall run the risk of lowering ourselves, even in the sight of those who hold us most dear. It is un-necessary to remind them that though we are goddesses at some times, we are but ordinary women at others.

The husband should always find the wife fresh, beautiful, sweet as a flower; but he should believe her to be so adorned by Nature, like the lilies of the field. It is just as well that he should not know that her beauty is acquired or preserved at the cost of a thousand little attentions, that he should

not suspect she possesses means of enhancing it—harmless means, I admit; but which
he might think foolish and ridiculous.

Some women may object that if all this
care is necessary, marriage must be slavery.
All I can say is, total disregard of appear-
ances and too much familiarity will make
an *inferno* of it.

What! shall we make a thousand efforts,
and submit to privations and constraints to
build up and establish a fortune, and shall
we take no trouble whatever to secure our
own happiness? Shall we command our
smiles, hide our feelings, and put on good
manners to please ordinary acquaintances and
strangers, and hesitate to cultivate refined
habits so as to retain for ever the heart of the
man whom we adore—or the woman (for this
concerns men, too), who holds their honour
and their happiness in her frail hands?

Face this question from my point of
view, and you will find it light and
easy to follow my advice, and to carry out

in detail the rules that I am about to give you.

But let us go back for a moment. I cannot conceive how a stout woman can so far forget herself as to appear before her husband in a short petticoat while dressing. If she does so, how can she wonder when she sees him admiring the slim forms of more graceful and slender women? I have seen a young woman tying up her scanty locks with a greasy string, so that they looked like a little tail or a broom, and then complain of the admiration that her husband showed at the sight of long and abundant hair on other women. My dear lady, you should hide your imperfections; this is not being false, but it is not necessary to display your defects. Perhaps at heart your husband was hurt by your indifference to please him, or to hide your little shortcomings from him. On such matters a man likes to be kept in the dark; and he is right. What is life, what is love, without some illusions?

B

I feel a great desire to tell the lords of creation that they can afford, even less than the fair sex, to lose the glamour with which the love of their *fiancées* has surrounded them, and that the inconsiderateness which men show under these circumstances is really culpable.

Everyone should do their utmost, and take as much, if not more, pains to preserve as to obtain love. This applies as much to the time after as before marriage, to the gifts of Nature as well as to those that have been acquired by art.

I flatter myself that in this connection the book I have written may be useful to virtuous women who wish to be happy, and also to bring happiness to the being who is dearest to them.

BARONNE STAFFE.

MORSANG-SUR-ORGE,
       March 21, 1891.

THE
LADY'S DRESSING-ROOM.

Part I.

THE DRESSING-ROOM.

Its Furnishing.

THE dressing-room of every well-bred woman should be both elegant and comfortable in proportion to her fortune and position; it may be simply comfortable if its owner cannot make it luxurious, but must be provided with everything necessary for a careful toilette.

Under the heading "The Bath-Room" I shall describe a dressing-room which also contains baths; but at this moment I wish to speak of the dressing-room alone.

The great ladies of the eighteenth century, whose ablutions were somewhat restricted, employed Watteau, Boucher,

Fragonard, and others, to paint their
dressing-rooms, wherein they received their
friends while they were themselves being
painted, powdered, and patched. In the
present day no one would dream of exposing
delicate fresco wall-paintings or beautiful
ceilings to the hot vapour and damp which
are necessitated by an abundant use of hot
and cold water.

Some dressing-rooms have their walls entirely covered with tiles—blue, pink, or pale
green. This tiling has the merit of being
bright and clean, but the effect is a little
cold to both sight and touch. Hangings
are generally preferred; they should be in
neutral tints or very undecided tones, so as
not to clash with the colours of the dresses.
Very often light or bright-coloured silks are
covered over with tulle or muslin, so as to
attenuate their vividness and at the same
time preserve their texture from the effect
of vapour.

Sometimes the walls are hung with

large-patterned cretonnes or coloured linens;
but cotton or linen stuffs are always a little
hard, and any very conspicuous pattern on
the walls is apt to detract from the effect of
the toilette, which should be the one thing
to attract the eye when its wearer is in the
room. Personally, I prefer a dressing-room
to be hung with sky-blue or crocus-lilac
under *point d'esprit* tulle. These hangings,
which will form an admirable background
to dresses of no matter what colour, should
be ornamented with insertions of lace.

The floor should be covered with a pearl-
grey carpet with a design of either roses or
lilac. From the centre of the ceiling should
hang a small lustre to hold candles; and
care should be taken to place wide *bobèches*
on these candles, so as to prevent any danger
of the wax falling on the dresses.

One or two large windows should light
this dressing-room. The ground-glass panes
should have pretty designs on them; and
double curtains of silk and tulle, the latter

edged with lace, should drape them volu-
minously.

Indispensable Accessories.

There must be two tables, opposite to
each other, of different dimensions, but the
same shape. The larger table is meant for
minor ablutions, and on it should be placed
a jug and basin, which should be chosen
with taste and care. The table is draped
to match the walls; above it should run a
shelf, on which are placed the bottles for
toilet waters and vinegars, dentifrices and
perfumes, the toilet bottle and glass, etc.
At either side of the basin should be placed
the brush and soap trays, the sponges, etc.

The other table, which is smaller, bears
the mirror, which should be framed in a
ruche of satin and lace; the table itself is
draped like its companion. As this table
is meant for the operation of hair-dressing,
everything necessary to that important art
must be found upon it. The various boxes

for pins and hair-pins; a large casket, in which are placed the brushes and combs, whose elegance should be on a par with that of the rest of the room; the bottles of perfume and of scented oil or pomades; the powder boxes; the manicure case, etc., should all have their places on this table, at either side of which should be fixed a couple of tall candelabra.

The fireplace should occupy the centre of the wall opposite the windows; a Dresden clock or a pretty bust in terra-cotta, with some vases of fresh flowers, is all that need be placed upon it. At one side of the fireplace should be placed a *chaise-longue* in blue or mauve damask, the pattern on it being in white; and here and there about the room a few arm-chairs and smaller ones of gilt cane will be found convenient.

At either side of the dressing-table there should be a wardrobe. One of these should have three mirrors in its doors, for the ordinary wardrobe with a single panel

of glass has been banished from all artistic
bed-rooms and dressing-rooms. The side
doors open at opposite angles, and thus
form a triple-sided, full-length mirror, in
which one can judge of the effect of both
dress and *coiffure* from all points of view.
The second wardrobe, which should be
lacquered like its companion, has no mirror,
its doors being painted with garlands of
flowers. In it are placed the reserve stock of
bran, starch, soaps, powder, creams, etc. etc.

No slop-buckets or water-cans should
be seen, nor should any dresses or other
paraphernalia be visible; everything of
that kind should be hidden from sight in
special closets or cupboards near at hand.
If the dressing-room does not adjoin the
bath-room, the tub, of which we shall speak
farther on, should be brought each day into
the dressing-room for the daily sponge bath,
which replaces the larger bath one may
have to go and take elsewhere, or which
may be forbidden on account of health.

A More Simple Dressing-Room.

A dressing-room, however, may be much more simple than this. All excess of luxury may be suppressed without preventing a woman of taste from making the little sanctuary of her charms both elegant and tasteful.

A pretty wall-paper should be chosen, and the floor covered with an oil-cloth. Drape the deal tables with wide flounces of cretonne edged with frills of the same material; cover the tables with linen toilet-cloths edged with deep thread lace, and on them place the washing utensils in bright coloured ware. If the tables are small, have shelves made—which you can cover in the same style as the tables—to accommodate the bottles and boxes, which should be chosen with care, to make up for their moderate price. If your mirror is somewhat ordinary, you can dissimulate its frame under a pleated frill, which you can fasten on with small tacks. You can ornament your

B*

wardrobe yourself, painting and varnishing it
to match the room, and to please your own
individual fancy. The slop-buckets and
the water-cans should be hidden under the
flounces of the tables.

If it is necessary to keep your dresses,
your band-boxes, your boots and shoes, etc.,
in your dressing-room, you should have some
shelves placed across the end of the room at
a sufficient height to allow you to hang
your dresses from hooks. On these shelves
you can put your boxes, parcels, etc.; the
whole being hidden by curtains to match
the draperies of the tables. These curtains
should not be placed against the wall, as
they would then reveal the outlines of all
the things they are meant to hide. They
should be hung from the ceiling, and enclose
the shelves as in an alcove; behind them
also may be placed the bath-tub, which is
not usually exposed to view. The great
matter in a dressing-room is to have one
large enough to be comfortable.

THE BATH-ROOM.

Its Arrangements and Appointments.

THE bath-room should be arranged according to the pecuniary resources at one's disposal; but here, as everywhere else, one should do one's best.

The millionaires of New York have sometimes bath-rooms worthy of Roman empresses. In Europe some very rich women, artists, and others whom it is unnecessary to mention, are particularly luxurious in everything that concerns the bath-room. The walls of these rooms are sometimes panelled with vari-coloured onyxes, framed in copper mouldings, which are polished every day. From the ceiling hang quaint chandeliers of rose or opalescent crystal; and a rich Oriental curtain, hanging from a golden rod, veils

the bath of rose-coloured marble. At the
opposite side of the room is placed a couch
covered with the skin of a Polar bear,
whereon, clad in a luxurious *peignoir*, one
reposes after the fatigues of the bath and
the *douche*. In one corner, also screened
from view by a silken curtain, are the
various apparatus for *douches*, shower, wave,
needle, or any other kind of spray bath
which may be desired. In the opposite
corner is placed the flat tub or sponge-bath
in porcelain. This immense basin is accom-
panied by another one of smaller dimensions,
and both are painted with designs of water-
lilies and aquatic plants. Near each bath is
handily placed taps for hot, cold, and tepid
water; and on small shelves of marble all
the articles one requires when bathing.

Utensils and Accessories.

When the bath-room has to serve at
the same time as a dressing-room, one must
place therein a large wash-stand with a

complete toilet set in porcelain ware or
silver, with all the minor articles to match.
There must, of course, be also the dressing-
table, which may be ornamented according to the taste of the presiding divinity.
Everything placed upon it—brushes, combs,
boxes, scent-bottles, etc.—should be chosen
with artistic taste. One must not forget to
mention the large wardrobe, with its three
doors of plate-glass mirror, such as I have
already mentioned. Therein are placed the
bath-linen, the flesh-gloves, loofahs, and all
the arsenal of feminine coquetry—creams,
cosmetics, perfumes, etc. etc.—which should
be hidden from every eye, as no one likes
to be suspected of adventitious aids. One
should not be able to see in this dressing-
room and bath-room combined either trinkets, dresses, laces, or ribbons. Jewels and
trinkets, as well as valuable laces, should be
kept in the bed-room, and all dresses put
out of sight in wardrobes or closets.

In many houses, however, the bath-room

is used by all the members of the family,
and can therefore not be treated as a
dressing-room.   Under such circumstances
it is not difficult to arrange a bath-room
from which all unnecessary luxury may be
banished while preserving every necessary
comfort.

It is best to paint the walls in oil colour
—with an imitation of marble, if you can get
it well done.   The floor should be covered
with linoleum, and the ground-glass windows should have the family monogram
engraved in the centre.   The various kinds
of baths should be ranged round the wall :
sitz-baths, sponge-baths, and the smaller
baths for children.   The taps of hot and
cold water should be placed over the large
bath, unless the water for it is heated by
means of a " geyser " ; and there should
also be a porcelain sink, into which the
smaller baths can be emptied.   Before each
bath, large or small, should be placed a
mat in cut-out leather, or, what is perhaps

better, in cork, whereon the bather may stand ; and near each bath, at a convenient level, shelves should be fastened to the wall to carry the necessary soaps and sponges.

In many bath-rooms where the water is heated in the room itself by means of some gas apparatus, the heater should contain a linen-box, for it is best to wrap oneself in hot linen on leaving a bath. The bath-heater must have a pipe leading into the outer air, to obviate the possibility of noxious fumes ; and with this pre-caution it is a useful thing, as it maintains the temperature in the bath-room.

A wardrobe should contain a supply of bath-linen, fine towels, Turkish towels, bath-sheets, etc.; herein are also placed on the shelves the various kinds of soaps, the boxes of starch, the bags of bran, the perfumes, almond paste, cold creams, car-bonate of soda, etc. etc. In one corner of the room should be placed the hand-lamp and aromatic perfume-box which are sometimes used in cases of illness for sweating-baths. There are certain kinds of portable apparatus for vapour-baths which can, if desired, be placed in the same room. These apparatus, and those for shower and "rain" baths, are generally hidden behind a curtain, which divides them off from the rest of the room.

Besides the actual baths, there should be in the bath-room a couch or ottoman, whereon to repose after the bath; a little table, in case one would wish to have a cup of tea; some chairs; and enough towel-horses whereon to lay out both the warm dry linen before the bath, as well as the wet linen after. It is unnecessary to place a dressing-table in such a bath-room as this : one returns to one's bed-room or dressing-room to complete one's toilette.

On Bathing.

Regular bathing should enter into the habits of all classes of society. If it is

absolutely impossible to immerse oneself
completely every day in a large bath, or if
it is forbidden by the doctor, a sponge-bath
may be considered sufficient for the needs
of cleanliness and health.

The human skin is a complicated network, whose meshes it is necessary to keep
free and open, so that the body may be
enabled through them to eliminate the
internal impurities, from which it is bound
to free itself, under pain of sickness,
suffering, and possible death. The healthy
action of the pores of the skin is stimulated
by the bath, especially if it is followed by
friction with a flesh-glove or a rough towel.
One can dispense with *massage* if one
objects to be manipulated by a strange
hand. Both fevers and contagious maladies
of many kinds are often avoided by such
simple precautions as these.

In cases of internal inflammation and
congestion, and of bilious colic, there is no
more certain remedy than a hot bath. It

is also known to have worked surprising
cures in cases of obstinate constipation.
Anyone who is afraid of having caught a
contagious malady should immediately have
recourse to a hot bath, as it is quite possible
that the infection may make its way out of
the body through the pores.   Of course,
particular care would be needed not to take
a chill on leaving the bath.

Cleanliness of the skin has a great effect
in the proper assimilation of nourishment
by the body ; and it has even been recognised that well-washed pigs yield superior
meat to those that are allowed to indulge
their propensities for wallowing in the mire.
It is therefore hardly necessary to repeat
that the salutary expulsion which the body
accomplishes through the skin, teaches the
necessity of keeping the pores open by
absolute cleanliness, the smallest particle of
grime or the finest dust being sufficient to
block the tiny openings with which Nature
has so admirably endowed the cuticle.

Pitiful Middle Ages that ignored the use of soap and water! "A thousand years without a bath!" cries Michelet in one of his historical works. It is not surprising that plagues and pestilences ravaged poor humanity in those days. Even in the time of Henri IV. the use of the bath must still have been sufficiently rare, when one remembers the *naïf* astonishment of a *grand seigneur* of the period who asked, "Why should one wash one's hands when one does not wash one's feet?"

Even at the Court of *Le Roi Soleil* the fair ladies were yet so neglectful on this point that one shudders with disgust when one reads about their habits; and yet in all ages *les grandes coquettes* have recognised the good effects of baths and ablutions. Isabel of Bavaria, having heard that Poppæa, wife of Nero, used to fill her bath of porphyry with asses' milk and the juice of strawberries, determined not to be behindhand in similar researches. Even

in those days marjoram was recommended,
and justly so, for its refreshing effect upon
the skin; so the spouse of Charles VII.
had enormous decoctions of this plant
prepared, in which to bathe.

It is on record that Anne Boleyn took
baths, a fact which is more or less supported by the story of certain of the
courtiers, who, by way of flattery, drank
her health in part of the water wherein
she had bathed. Diane de Poictiers bathed
every morning in a bath of rain-water.

In the eighteenth century the great
ladies became fanciful in the matter of
baths, and had them concocted, like
Poppæa, of asses' milk; of *eau de mouron*,
like Isabel; of milk of almonds; of *eau de
chair*, or weak veal-broth; of water distilled from honey and roses; of melon-
juice; of green-barley water; of linseed-
water, to which was added balm of Mecca,
rendered soluble with the yolk of an egg.
All these decoctions were undoubtedly

good for the skin, but the bath for
cleansing purposes does not need so much
preparation.

The Dauphine Marie Antoinette "invented for her *demi-bain*," says a writer of
her time, "a half-bath which yet bears her
name." It was a deep basin of oblong
shape, mounted in a wooden frame supported on legs, the back of the frame being
raised and stuffed like the back of an
armchair. This shape is more conveniently
imitated in zinc at present. For her large
baths the Princess had a decoction prepared
of *serpolet*, laurel leaves, wild thyme, and
marjoram, to which was added a little sea-
salt. The prescription for these baths was
made by Fagon, chief physician to Louis
XIV., who also desired that they should be
taken cold in winter and tepid in summer,
so as to balance the external temperature
with the sensibility of the epidermis.

Hot, Cold, and Sponge Baths.

There are many people who immerse
themselves every day for a few instants in
a cold bath; one must be very strong to
support this form of bath, and it is perhaps
wiser not to try it without having con-
sulted a doctor.   Even when the cold bath
is allowed, it is best to take only one plunge
and come out at once. The water ought to be
about 50° to 60° Fahrenheit, and a good rubbing is indispensable after a bath of this kind.

The hot bath is good for those who are
subject to a rush of blood to the head.   Its
temperature should not exceed 100°.

The tepid bath is the one most used,
and its temperature may range from 68° to
96°.   It is a mistake to remain too long in
a tepid bath; thirty minutes is the maximum time one should stay therein, and it
is perhaps best to leave it after a quarter of
an hour, unless of course medical orders
decide otherwise.

If it is impossible, for various reasons, to have a large bath every day, a sponge bath will replace it conveniently, and is sufficient for the necessities of health and cleanliness. One should begin by taking a sponge bath of tepid water, and then by degrees one can lower the temperature of the water until at·last the daily tub is a cold one. In all cases, however, the bath-room should be slightly warmed in winter, spring, and autumn; and care should be taken that the towels are warm and dry. People with delicate lungs should remain faithful to the warm bath. A good rubbing is a necessity after all and every bath; but of that we shall speak farther on, as well as of *massage*. It is often a good thing to take a little air and exercise after the bath, but only on condition of walking very fast. Never take a bath, or in any way immerse yourself in water, immediately after having eaten; a bath would be distinctly dangerous, and even minor ablutions are apt to trouble the

digestion.   One should allow three hours
to elapse between any meal at all copious
and a bath.

When soap is used in a large bath, it
should be used towards the end of the time
of immersion, and should be immediately
washed off with clear water.   In a sponge
bath this is an easy matter, as the fresh
water is ready to hand in a large basin
alongside of the bath.   The soap chosen
should be white and very pure, and little,
if at all, perfumed.   It seems almost superfluous to say that it is contrary to cleanliness and hygiene that two people should
bathe in the same water, no matter how
healthy they may be; but as some fond
mothers have a habit of taking their little
ones into the bath with them, it is as well
to warn them that the delicate skin of
babies is often apt to suffer from such a
custom.

Soothing and Refreshing Baths.

It is unnecessary here to speak of Russian or Turkish baths, nor even of vapour baths. These last belong properly to the domain of the doctor, who can order or administer them when necessary. The others demand an installation which it is almost impossible to have at home, even when expense is no object.

But there are other baths whose soothing properties may be recommended without having recourse to a doctor. In spring it is best to take one's bath at night, just before going to bed, so as to avoid all possibility of a chill, which is more dangerous at that time of year than any other, and also so that the skin may benefit by the moist warmth which it will thus be able to keep for several hours after having left the water. A delicious bath for this season can be prepared with cowslips or wild primroses. Three handfuls of these flowers,

freshly gathered, should be thrown into the
bath, which thus becomes not only delightfully perfumed, but extremely calming to
the nerves by the virtue in the sweet
golden petals.

The bath of strawberries and raspberries
which Madame Tallien took every morning,
as we are told by the gossips of her time,
was prepared in the following manner:—
Twenty pounds of strawberries and two of
raspberries were crushed and thrown into
the bath, from which the bather emerged
with a skin freshly perfumed, soft as velvet,
and tinged with a delicate pink.

A bath of lime-flowers (also a delightful perfume) is particularly soothing to
over-excited nerves. A decoction of spinach,
if a sufficient quantity were obtained, would
make an excellent bath for the skin. Here,
however, is a recipe equally good for rendering
the skin fresh and delicate :—Sixty grammes
of glycerine and one hundred grammes of
rose-water, mixed with two quarts of water,

are added to the bath five minutes before using it. Some women mix almond-paste with their bath, and perfume it with violet; others prefer oatmeal and orange-flower water; others, again, prefer tincture of benzoin, which gives the water a milky appearance. Nothing is better for the skin than a bran bath. Two pounds of bran, placed in a muslin bag, are allowed to soak in a small quantity of water for three hours before the bath, to which it is added, is required. A bath of aromatic salts is easily prepared. Pound into powder some carbonate of soda and sprinkle it with some aromatic essences (of which only a small quantity is needed). These aromatic essences can be prepared beforehand, according to the following recipe :—

Essence of fine lavender	...	15 grammes
Essence of rosemary	...	10 „
Essence of eucalyptus	...	5 „
Carbonate of soda crystals	...	600 „

Pound the crystals, sprinkle and mix them

with the essences, and keep them in a well-stoppered bottle. For a large bath, 315 grammes of this aromatic salt will be required; for a basin. a teaspoonful to a quart of water.

For a tonic and refreshing effect upon the skin the aromatic bath is one of the best: 500 grammes of the various aromatic plants enumerated in Fagon's recipe for Marie Antoinette's bath (of which I have already spoken) should be allowed to infuse for an hour in three quarts of boiling water; the water should then be strained, and added to the bath. Another bath which is both strengthening and soothing is thus composed :—Dissolve in the bath half a pound of crystals of carbonate of soda, two handfuls of powdered starch, and a teaspoonful of essence of rosemary; the temperature of the bath should be 36° to 37° C., and the immersion should last from fifteen to twenty minutes.

When the nervous system is much

exhausted, the following bath will be found useful, viz., an ounce of ammonia to a bucket of water. In a bath of this kind the flesh becomes as firm and smooth as marble, and the skin is purified in the most perfect way. It would be unkind to finish this section on baths without remembering those who suffer from rheumatism, to whom I can recommend the following bath as likely to ease them from their pain. A concentrated emulsion should be made with 200 grammes of soft soap and 200 grammes of essence of turpentine ; it should be well shaken together, until the mixture is in a lather. For a bath, take half this emulsion, which has an agreeable smell of pine when mixed with the water. After five minutes' immersion in a warm bath thus prepared, the patient is aware of a distinct diminution of pain, and a pleasant warmth spreads all over the body. At the end of a quarter of an hour he feels a slight pricking sensation, which is not at all unpleasant ;

and he should then leave the bath, and get straight into bed, where he will at once fall asleep; on waking in the morning he will find his pain greatly alleviated.

Massage and Rubbings.

Massage comes from the Greek word *masso*, "I knead." The *masseur* or *masseuse* kneads with the hands all the muscular parts of the body, works the articulations to make them supple, and excites the vitality of the skin. This custom has come to us from the East, where it has been known since the days of antiquity. The Romans employed it greatly. In the Russian form of massage, the hand of the operator is covered with a well-soaped glove; and sometimes the kneading of the body is followed by a slight flagellation with birch twigs. Massage must follow the bath, and not precede it. When the skin is moist with water or vapour, it is naturally more supple and flexible, and is

therefore more easily kneaded. The patient
feels a great fatigue at the end of the
operation, but this is soon followed by a
sense of well-being and vivacity. Care
should be taken, however, not to make an
abuse of massage—for if it is over-done,
its effects are exhausting rather than
strengthening; but in certain climates,
and in certain maladies, there is no doubt
it is very beneficial. In many cases
judicious rubbings are an excellent sub-
stitute for massage, and are rendered all
the more easy by the various modern
inventions which help one to apply friction
to the back and sides. It is best to use
for these frictions a flesh-glove or a broad
band made of horse-hair, coarse wool, or
rough linen. It is called a "dry-rubbing"
when applied alone. Nothing is better,
after a foot-bath or a sponge-bath, than a
vigorous rubbing; it increases the force
and vigour of the body, benefits the general
health, and consequently is an admirable

aid to beauty. After the dry-rubbing, all the body should be rubbed with a piece or a band of flannel dipped in toilet-vinegar or perfume.

Sea-Bathing—River-Bathing.

It is not well to take a sea-bath either the day of, nor the day after, one's arrival at a watering-place. It is best to exclude from one's diet wine, coffee, and spirits, and to allow one's organisation time to absorb the ozone of the salt sea-air. The best moment for a bath is high tide: at low tide, or when the tide is coming in or going out, there are certain drawbacks which it would take too long to explain here. One should never enter the sea unless three hours have elapsed since the last meal, so that the digestive organs may be in complete repose.

It is unwise to bathe if one happens to be very much excited, if one is suffering from any acute or chronic malady, if one

has had a sleepless night, or if one has been
undergoing any violent exercise. One should
undress slowly, and, once in one's bathing
costume, and wrapped in a cloak, it is a
good thing to walk a little on the beach, so
that the body may be warmed by exercise,
and therefore better able to resist the
shock on entering the cold water. Delicate
women and children who suffer from cold
feet even in summer, would do well to take
off their sandals for a few minutes before
entering the sea, so as to warm their feet
and ankles on the sun-baked sand; and
such persons will find it is advisable to
take a few drops of Malaga or port before
entering the sea.

It is best to go rapidly into the water,
so that the whole body may be immersed
in as short a time as possible, care being
taken, however, to cover up the hair
carefully, as there is nothing so disastrous
in effect to a woman's hair as sea-water.
Unless one is strong, the bath should be a

c

short one, and a few minutes' immersion
is sufficient. On leaving the water, one
should again be wrapped up in one's cloak
and return slowly to one's cabin, where it is
best to stand in a pan of warm water while
one is drying one's body. If the hair is
damp, it should be rubbed dry at once, and
then, if necessary, allowed to float loosely
on the shoulders for half an hour. Open-
air exercise should be considered a necessity
after a sea-bath.

As to children, it is extremely dangerous
to bathe them in the sea before they are at
least two years old; and even at that age,
if the waves frighten them, they should not
be plunged in the water. A little baby has
not sufficient nervous force for the necessary
vigorous reaction, without which immersion
is harmful; his little body would be chilled,
and he would be exposed to the danger of
internal convulsions. A child should never
be forced to undergo the shock of a wave if
he is frightened thereby, as nothing is more

unwholesome than to bathe during violent
emotion; and there is no more violent
emotion than terror. It is best, therefore,
to give him a salt-water bath at home, and
then let him run and roll on the sand and
shingle, and paddle with his little feet in
the sea-pools; he will thus take a bath of
sunshine and salt sea-air, which will probably be much better for him, and he will
thus get accustomed little by little to the
sound and the force of the waves, whose
attraction he will not long resist, if he is
not frightened at the outset.

River-bathing has many attractions for
young and vigorous persons, and is very
strengthening to delicate individuals who
venture on it under proper conditions.
Even when strong and vigorous, it is not
well to unduly prolong a fresh-water bath,
as anything of fatigue is likely to bring on
cramp, than which there is nothing more
dangerous. One should not embark on this
sport without being well acquainted with

the currents of the river, and one can always find some intelligent native to give one the necessary indications.

River-bathing should be surrounded with exactly the same precautions as sea-bathing. After a storm one should abstain from the bath, as the water of the river will be soiled and muddy; and it is as well also not to bathe on the chilly rainy days with which we are unfortunately familiar even in summer.

Hydropathy and Hydropathic Appliances.

Hydropathy is a system of treatment of maladies (especially chronic ones) by the exclusive use of cold water in various forms Baths and *douches* of course form part of it; and besides these, the sick person is undressed, wrapped up in blankets on a couch, and made to drink innumerable glasses of cold water. Perspiration naturally follows, and he is then given either a cold bath or is enveloped in damp sheets. It is unwise,

however, to attempt this method of cold
applications within and without, unless
under the advice of a competent doctor,
this treatment requiring a considerable
amount of practical experience. Above
all, the water should be of a uniform
temperature—not more than 46° F., nor
less than 43°; the exact temperature is
46°. It is not by any means easy to obtain
this undeviating, unvarying temperature of
46°; but one can always find it at the
hydropathic establishment of Divonne,
which is situated between the mountains
of the Jura and the Lake of Geneva.
There several springs unite and form a
torrent, which in its turn joins that of the
mountain. It is this water which is used for
the baths and for all the different methods
of treatment of the establishment. After a
few baths, which are followed by vigorous
rubbings, one feels a sensation of warmth
and comfort, a sort of expansion of the
body, wherein the vital principle seems to

be born anew. The temperature of the
water at 46° seems icy to the body, whose
warmth is 98°; and on the first plunge
into the bath one can hardly tell whether
the water is icy cold or scalding hot, and
one has a stinging sensation as if one were
whipped with nettles. The immersion
should only last two minutes, and on
leaving the water one should be well
rubbed down with some rough woollen
stuff. Pleasant warmth soon returns, and
remains if one takes some exercise, or if one
is wrapped up in blankets.

One need not be afraid of catching cold
by the sudden plunge into icy water the
very moment one leaves one's bed. The
body has not time to lose its natural
warmth, and the violent shock of the cold
water only gives a stinging, prickling
sensation, which brings the blood almost
immediately in a rush to the surface, and
obviates all possibility of chill. Not only
is there no risk of catching cold, but very

often one can stop and cure a cold at the beginning by the use of hydropathy.

Though this cold-water treatment sounds very alarming, most people, even delicate women, who try it, become passionately attached to it, and have the necessary apparatus established in their own houses. One of the most appreciated forms of *douche* is that which is called the "crinoline," a circular one, as its name implies, which brings a fine rain to bear on the whole body at the same time, and about which the lady *habituées* of Divonne express themselves in enthusiastic terms. In fact, all these different forms of cold-water treatment are liked by women in general, on account of the benefit their nerves derive from their calming and strengthening effects.

Another method is called "packing," and thoroughly deserves its name. The patient is made up like a parcel—first in a wet sheet, over which are placed two woollen blankets, a quilt, and an eider-down counterpane. These are wrapped tightly round the body of the patient, who, thus bound hand and foot like a mummy, is very soon in a state of profuse perspiration. The coverings are then removed, and the patient plunged in the cold bath. The effect is prompt, soothing, and beneficial.

There is no denying that the science of medicine has found in hydropathy a puissant ally wherewith to vanquish chronic maladies, which before its discovery were often declared incurable. Feminine coquetry has also become aware of the beneficial effect of the cold-water treatment, for the brusque transitions of temperature, followed by the reactions which bring back the warmth to the surface of the body, revive the functions of the skin, strengthen the muscles, and soothe the nerves, all of which result in an increase of beauty in the feminine patient. Of course, to obtain the full benefit of hydropathic treatment, it is necessary to go

to some such establishment as that at
Divonne; but there are many forms of
hydropathic apparatus which it is quite
easy to establish in one's own house.
Baths, *douches*, needle-baths, "packing,"
rubbing, and *massage*—all these are perfectly possible to attain at home with a
certain amount of fitting-up. This is why
mention has been made of hydropathic
apparatus when speaking of the bath-room.
There are three kinds of *douches*—ascending,
descending, and horizontal. In the two
latter the reservoir must be placed at a fair
height, and the pipe should be of a good
size, so that the column of water may be
strong and voluminous. These are the
more common forms of *douches*. In the
ascending *douche* the reservoir is placed at
a lower level, and the pipe should be small
in diameter.

How to Clean Sponges.

Nothing is so horrible and disgusting as a sponge that looks grey and dingy, even if it be not really dirty.

A sponge in this state should be steeped in milk for twelve hours. After this time rinse it in cold water, and it will be as good as new, *minus* the expense. Lemon-juice is also excellent for whitening a sponge.

Sponges always become greasy and sticky at last, and no amount of soap and water will make them fit to use when they get into this state. Hydrochloric acid must then be used, and a teaspoonful of this in a pint of water will be enough to take out the grease and clean the sponge. One may also have recourse at first to carbonate of soda, which sometimes proves sufficient. These are small but very important details, over which the mistress of the house should herself keep watch, for servants think them unworthy of their attention.

Part II.

THE GENERAL CARE OF THE BODY.

Cleanliness of the Body.

"CLEANLINESS is half a virtue, and unclean-
liness is a vice and a half," says Alexandre
Dumas, and this is not saying enough.
Want of cleanliness is an ugly and ignoble
vice, and it is marvellous that women above
all should lay themselves open to such a
reproach, for it is incompatible with their
desire to be beautiful and beloved.

It was in the darkness of the Middle
Ages that people dared to condemn cleanliness as a baleful remnant of ancient times
(times when humanity, being more civilised,
practised the use of baths and ablutions);
it was in the gloom of those centuries that

this virtue was looked upon as an impiety. The impiety, on the contrary, consists in not taking care of one's body, that body which ought to be daily freed from every speck or stain which the conditions of life impose upon it in our present state of existence.

Even now young girls leave convents and large schools with inadequate notions of cleanliness, and this is inconceivable; and even when they return home, their mothers systematically neglect to instruct them in that part of hygiene which consists in those habits of neatness and daintiness which they themselves have only gradually acquired—sometimes, indeed, not without humiliation.

The Romans washed their bodies before going into the Temple. All Eastern religions, we may observe, order ablutions before prayer. Does not this rule, as hygienic as it is religious, show plainly that physical purity should go hand-in-hand with moral purity? The Koran incessantly recommends the use of baths. Shall we, then, who are in so many ways above Orientals, be content to remain so much below them in these all-important matters? In these times of ultra-civilisation, shall we continue to ignore the most elementary rules of the dignity of humanity? The animals, which do not possess our hands with a separate thumb, and have none of our facilities for care and neatness, clean their bodies, brighten up their fur or their plumage, from a natural instinct; and shall man, who is their king by his reason and divine intelligence, neglect his body? And shall woman, that marvel of creation, suffer her satin skin, with its pearly reflections, to be profaned by any impurity? Surely not; and therefore the whole human body should be purified every night and every morning from any stain or impurity it may have received under the animal and material laws to which it is still in subjection.

As long as we are not ethereal spirits, as long as we have to live as mortals, we should submit ourselves to our condition, doing all that is in our power to ameliorate it.

And indeed cleanliness already brings us a step nearer to the angels of light; while slovenliness, on the other hand, keeps us down in the depths of our original mire.

Cleanliness is as indispensable to health as it is to beauty.

A woman who keeps the pores of her skin open by the daily and abundant use of cold or tepid water, will keep well and grow old slowly. But under the closed pores of a skin not well or frequently washed the flesh becomes flabby and soft.

A well-washed skin is smooth, silky, and fresh; but if repeated layers of perspiration and dust are allowed to accumulate, the skin becomes dry and feverish.

But for numbers of people, it may be

argued, it is not possible to take baths every day; the time and the means to do so are not at their disposal. To this I reply that a sponge-bath, which is quite sufficient as regards cleanliness, only requires a few moments of time and a quiet corner. If one cannot spare these few moments every day to take an entire bath, at least one might take time for a partial one, certain parts of the body requiring more care than others. Then, one or twice a week at the least, the necessary time for taking a complete bath should be made. This is the very *minimum* of washing that our bodies absolutely require. As for the *maximum* of cleanliness, it is impossible to fix it, for there can be no limit on this point. There are people so scrupulously clean that they purify their stomachs and intestines by swallowing a large glass of hot or cold water every morning, according to their state of health; others have recourse to the classic instrument of Molière, simply as a means of cleanliness. It is easy to imagine that they are quite as much concerned with the care of their outer being.

The slightest negligence on this point is altogether inexcusable. We are wanting in self-respect if we fail to keep our person rigorously clean and neat. And Nature will quickly punish us for such neglect by sickness and premature old age. Bathing and washing, assisted by good soaps, and even vinegars and perfumes, will make our bodies firm, fit, and capable of endurance. Water has the virtue of dissipating all fatigue, destroying the germs of illness, and by giving us pure bodies it renders our souls also more pure. " A healthy spirit in a healthy body."

THE FACE.

Ablutions of the Face.

It is admitted, then, that to exercise
their functions properly the pores of the
skin should be kept open, and that washing
is the best means of keeping them free from
the secretions or accumulations which might
obstruct and clog them.

It is, therefore, as contrary to the rules
of hygiene and coquetry as to that of
cleanliness to abstain (as Patti has been
accused of doing) from ever washing the
face.

At the same time, there are some precautions to be taken on this subject.

If you have a red face, you should use
hot water ; it will send the blood away, and
stop the congestion caused by the rush of

blood to the parts affected. It is also bad to wash in cold water when the weather is very warm, or when the face is very much heated either by natural or artificial warmth. Tepid water should be used, with lotions, but without soap. The face should then be slightly powdered, and allowed to dry without being wiped. The same treatment applies when the weather is very dry.

The face should be dried, very gently, with a very fine and rather worn towel. Rough friction with a hard towel will have the effect of thickening the skin. It would be well to remember that the face requires as delicate care as a precious piece of porcelain or a fine work of art. The face, for instance, should never be bathed in too violent a manner, such as plumping the head into a great basin of water. Neither should the face be too constantly washed over and over again in the course of the day, at all moments. One celebrated beauty has never made use of anything but her own hand with which to wash her face. She dries it with a light and very soft flannel. Another beauty prefers a sponge.

We are told that one of the prettiest of our women in society plunges a towel into very hot water, wrings it out, and lays it on her face, where she keeps it for about half-an-hour. She goes through this performance at night, before getting into bed, wiping off lightly with the humidity produced on the surface of the skin any dust that may have collected there during the day. This lady has no wrinkles.

A woman of fifty whose skin is as smooth as that of a young girl has never washed her face except with extremely hot water, which, she declares, tightens the skin and destroys wrinkles. One of this lady's friends washes with cold water immediately after the hot (Russian fashion), and her sister washes with hot water at night and cold in the morning.

These are rather contradictory counsels;

but all these apparent contradictions no
doubt depend on the state of the skin in
these different persons. I will add the
advice of a physician : in winter wash your
face with cold water, in summer with warm
or tepid water, so as to keep in harmony
with the external temperature. Hard
water which will not dissolve soap is bad
for all ablutions, especially for those of the
face. If it is impossible to obtain rain- or
river-water, at least soften the hard water
by means of a little borax or a few drops of
ammonia.

The spirituous essences which are often
added to the water for washing the face
are very destructive to it. Frequent applications of alcohol dry and harden the skin,
and consequently prevent it from perform-
ing its proper functions or from nourishing
itself with the fresh air or the damp
atmosphere.

On the other hand, it is advisable not
to expose the face to the air immediately

after washing it. When the pores have just been opened by the use of water, the skin should be protected from the action of the air, or it will become coarsened and chapped. Half an hour should be allowed to pass before going out, sitting at an open window, etc. It is for this reason that women who do not occupy themselves much with their household concerns prefer to wash their faces just before going to bed.

It may sometimes be necessary to use soap for the face. In this case the soap (of which we shall speak later) should be very carefully chosen, and it is well not to use it more than is really necessary, and never when the weather is very warm.

Lemon-juice cleans the skin very well, and is much better than soap. Strawberry-juice has the same detergent action, and is, moreover, very good for the skin. Rain-water is better than any Turkish bath for washing the face. Enveloped from head to foot in a waterproof, encounter the downpour or the soft rain of heaven without an umbrella, exposing your face to it during an hour's walk. The rain and the dampness of the air will not only soften and wash the tissues perfectly, but they will efface also from the skin the little lines made there by the dryness of the artificial heating of rooms. Quiet, and sufficient sleep, and walks in the rain, are said to have been the sole beauty-philtres used by Diana de Poitiers, who went out every day, no matter what the weather was, and who used no umbrella, for the good reason that they had not yet at that time been re-invented from the Romans.

The Complexion—Colour.

All women who belong to the white race have always concerned themselves, and will always concern themselves, about the purity, freshness, and brilliancy of their complexion. And in truth a beautiful colour, a white and fine skin, form one of the great attractions of a woman, who cannot be pronounced perfectly beautiful if there is any defect in her complexion.

It is generally thought that the colour and texture of the skin can be improved by outward applications, and this is to a great extent an error. The complexion, of whatever kind it is, depends mainly on the state of the health, on the constitution or the temperament. It is clear, then, that we must have recourse to hygiene rather than to cosmetics in order to diminish the faults of colour.

There are families in which a fine complexion is transmitted as a heritage. You may be sure that such a race is healthy, and has pure blood, which has never been tainted by any of those atrocious diseases which desolate humanity. A celebrated beauty was once asked the secret of the rose-leaf tint of her cheeks and the delicacy of her blue-veined skin. "Robust and virtuous ancestors," was her laconic reply.

Nothing is less desirable from the point of view either of health or æsthetics than a face too highly coloured, especially if the roses extend all, or nearly all, over the whole of it. It indicates a plethoric habit. People afflicted with this very high colour, whose eyes even are bloodshot, are generally, it may be noticed, large eaters and lovers of ease and luxury, and have a great repugnance to healthy exercise. It is evident that to lower the tone of their complexion these people should restrain their appetites, choose less succulent foods, deny themselves some of their comforts, and keep their over-nourished bodies a little under. They would at once find their health benefited by such *régime*, and their headaches, confusion of mind, and dizziness would disappear. Instead of being red all over, their complexion would change to the brilliant stage, which is a totally different thing, for even very bright roses are not out of place on the cheeks only, and then they make the forehead, nose, and chin, which they have happily forsaken, appear all the fairer. A brilliant feverish colour which shows itself on the cheek-bone only, is too often an indication of consumption. Unfortunately, it is not to hygiene alone that we must have recourse in such cases.

When the complexion is muddy, pale, pasty, too white, greenish, yellow, or purple, it always proclaims a bad state of health. Sometimes a muddy complexion is natural, but much more often it denotes dyspepsia, languid circulation, etc.

A pale colour is due to an indoor life without exercise, from the habit or the necessity of shunning the daylight and the sunshine. A pasty colour belongs to a lymphatic temperament. An olive complexion is not always a sign of ill-health; those who have it should look back and see whether they have not had some Southern or Creole ancestor before making themselves uneasy on the subject. A very white complexion, without any colour, belongs to persons seriously attacked in their health, though there is at times nothing else to show this. A purple colour may be produced by heart disease ; a yellow one needs quite special attention.

Thus we see that whenever the complexion is defective, care and precaution should always be taken.

Hygiene may often suffice, and we shall endeavour to trace the great outlines of this preventive remedy for the use of women at least.

A very thin woman may be in good health, but she never has a good complexion, according to the proverb which says "there is no beautiful skin over the bones." But presently we shall show her the means of growing a little fatter. We may, however, tell her and all women at once that it is necessary to restrain their impatience and irritability, which dry up the blood more than illness or even sorrow itself.

Everybody may be recommended to preserve the face from too great artificial heat.

Cold is unfavourable to dark complexions, and heat to fair ones. The wind makes the face either blueish or pale. Whenever it is possible to choose a walk, going against the wind should be avoided. Many parents dislike seeing their children kissed frequently, for the velvety skin of a baby suffers much therefrom. Too much kissing is bad for the complexion.

Further on we shall explain to women how they should live, and what they should eat, in order to preserve or improve a pretty colour, and how to remain beautiful while keeping their health.

Wrinkles.

There would be fewer wrinkles if people would correct themselves of certain bad habits. Repeated frowning leaves an indelible mark, in certain straight lines between the eyebrows. Lifting the eyebrows at every movement for nothing at all is done at the cost of long horizontal lines across the forehead, which makes people look five years older than they really are. A stereotyped artificial smile stamps two large creases from the nose to the corners of the mouth. Sitting up late at night reading novels is infallible for drawing that terrible network of crows' feet round the eyes which disfigures the prettiest face.

People who laugh a great deal have little wrinkles on their cheeks close to the mouth, but these are rather pleasing. There need be no anxiety except about wrinkles that come from causes we ought to fight against: cheerfulness is a virtue to be encouraged. Suffering traces lines on worn features, but they disappear with the return of health.

To delay the appearance of wrinkles, and to reduce the heaviness of the chin, the face should be washed and dried from the lower part up to the top. To avoid the dreaded crows' feet, wash the eyes in the direction from the temple towards the nose.

It is an immense mistake to fill up with face powder the lines made by wrinkles; it only makes them the deeper.

Some of the millionaires in New York, whose skins suffer from the over-heated rooms, have their faces sprayed with soft water for a quarter of an hour every night before going to bed. This has the effect of a very fine rain, which effaces the wrinkles and produces the required humidity for the epidermis. To counteract the disastrous effects of the dry and burning heat of stoves and *calorifères*, it is indispensable to stand vessels full of water on them, that the evaporation may render the air damp enough. Even better results may be obtained by using wet cloths, and renewing them as often as necessary.

The fear of wrinkles leads many women

to submit to the hardest sacrifices, in the
hope of conjuring away the demon of old
age.

Here is the manner in which one woman
in society proceeds to efface the signs which
late hours and gaieties leave on her face.
When she feels knocked up and in the
blues, if something has gone wrong or
worried her, she goes to bed and stays
there till her fatigue has passed off, or her
irritation is over and her good-humour
come back. Then she gets up, fresh, beautiful, in an amiable frame of mind, and all
her wrinkles smoothed out. She declares
that if all idle women followed her example
in the like circumstances, they would prolong their youth and beauty, calm their
nerves, and thus gain a desirable equanimity
of character.

A mother, careful of the beauty of her
daughter, tried the following treatment for
her during her first season. The young
lady went to a ball every day in the week,

but on Sundays she stayed in bed, only
rising in time for five o'clock tea and
retiring again at an early hour. The
results of this kind of life were happy.
The young girl did not catch cold once
during the season, and when the time came
for going to the seaside, she seemed to be
the only one who did not need any of the
benefits which society women expect from
the sea air. She was like a country girl,
and as fresh as a rose.

Women who have no children, and are
deprived of the immense joys and many
and arduous duties of maternity, would do
well to spend their leisure in perfecting
their own characters and hearts. Once
again, I would persuade all women that the
moral character is quite as—or, indeed, much
more—worthy of interest than the physical
body.

Far better have one wrinkle more, and
acquire a good quality, than a smooth forehead and the faults of a child.

Nevertheless if it is possible to take a moment of respite from the accomplishment of daily duties, I would urge a little rest for the face, four or five times a day, by shutting the eyes and remaining perfectly still for one, two, or five minutes, when it can be done without neglecting anything important. Even these short rests from occupations and agitations will greatly retard the ravages that time and life imprint on the face.

Sunburn.

You are no doubt justly annoyed, dear reader, when your jasmine-tinted complexion is burnt after walking in the hot sun or sitting for a long time on the beach.

But it is easy to restore to your face the pearly whiteness of which you were justly proud.

Bathe it in the evening with a cold infusion of fresh cucumbers cut up in slices in milk. A decoction of tansy in butter-

milk is still more efficacious. Butter-milk
by itself even will be of some use.

Another certain means of getting rid of
the burning caused by sea or country air
consists in washing with the juice of green
grapes, which can be obtained as follows:—
Wet your bunch of grapes, and sprinkle them
lightly with alum; then wrap them up in
white paper, and put them to cook under hot
charcoal embers. When the grapes are
tender, they will be sufficiently done. Take
off the paper, and squeeze the bunch under
a vessel to press out the juice, and wash
your face with this juice. You must perform this operation three times over at
intervals of four-and-twenty hours, but it is
an infallible remedy.

Many people believe, and not without
reason, that it blackens the skin to wash at
midday in summer. The hour of noon
should be dreaded by those who have delicate skins.

A foreign physician affirms that the

D

electric light burns the faces of those exposed to it, as much as the sun does. And
the moon—even the pale moon—is supposed
to have the same effect upon our skin.
After all, it is said to eat away stone; so
it may well have some effect upon our
complexions. The Maréchale d'Aumont,
"as beautiful in her old age as in her
youth," was in mortal fear of the night-
dew and the moon.

But let us return to the misdeeds of the
sun. The Italians proceed very simply
when they wish to remedy the effects of the
sun or of the sea air after a sojourn in their
country villas or on the borders of the
Adriatic, the Mediterranean, or the lakes,
in this wise : —They take the white of an
egg beaten into a good froth, bathe the face
with it, and leave it to dry on the skin for
a quarter of an hour, then rinse it off with
fresh water. This is done three or four
times, and always at night, just before
getting into bed. This last injunction, and

also that of drying the face gently with a very fine towel, are essential. I have already given the reasons for both. Finally, a mixture of lemon-juice and glycerine in equal parts has good results against the injuries done to our epidermis by the sun and the wind. If the skin will not bear glycerine—of which more later on—it should be replaced by rose-water.

Freckles.

Freckles are the despair of blonde and florid women especially, but also of brunettes who possess a white skin. Some doctors attribute these spots to the presence of a certain amount of iron in the blood. It has been proved that the abuse of ferruginous medicines is often the determinating cause of these yellow stains which spoil many a beautiful forehead.

Others say that freckles indicate a delicate constitution and a slow and feeble

circulation. The following are remedies
for these annoying spots :—

1st. One of my friends found the
following mixtures beneficial, with one
or other of which she anointed her freckles
every night, going to bed : one part of
tincture of iodine and three parts of
glycerine. 2nd. In half a pint of oil of
turpentine dissolve 7 grammes of powdered
camphor, then add 2 grammes of oil of sweet
almonds. This is an excellent liniment
for the inconvenience of which we
are now speaking. 3rd. 28 grammes of
powdered camphor and 112 grammes of
pure olive oil, melted by a gentle heat.
4th. Try applications of butter-milk, which
is as good as, if not better than, the foregoing
recipes. 5th. In some countries the perfumed water extracted from the iris by
means of steam (*bain-marie*) is used to
beautify the skin and complexion; if a
little salt of tartar is dissolved in this,
it will. remove freckles. 6th. Dissolve 16

centigrammes of borax in 20 grammes of rose-water and the same quantity of orange-flower water, and bathe the spots with this lotion. 7th. Fresh beans boiled in water, mashed and applied as a poultice, will produce an excellent effect. 8th. Mix vinegar, lemon-juice, alcohol, oil of lavender, oil of roses, oil of cedar, and distilled water; use this lotion going to bed, and wash with fresh water the next morning. 9th. Use recipe No. 1 for curing redness in the nose. 10th. A mixture formed of two parts juice of watercress and one part honey is much recommended for freckles and sunburn. The two substances, when mixed, should be passed through muslin, and rubbed in night and morning.

A few very simple precautions may prevent the appearance of freckles. Our ancestors, who were most careful of their complexions, wore masks of velvet in winter to protect their skin from the cold; in summer they wore silk masks to defend

their delicate epidermis against Apollo's
darts, which produce these hateful spots.
If it is impossible to revive the use of
masks, wear straw-coloured veils in April,
when the buds begin to star the meadows,
and spots unfortunately begin to blossom
on faces. It would be too long to explain
scientifically why you will be as safe from
the rays of the sun under yellow gauze as
under a mask, but I will answer for the
efficacy of this device. It may be objected
that straw-coloured veils are hardly becoming. The question is whether you care
most for the admiration of the people you
meet out of doors (who are often unknown
to you), or for that of the people who see
you at home with your face uncovered—your
friends, and, above all, your husband.

While travelling the face should be
only washed at night, and add to the water
for use a few drops of tincture of benzoin.
Lait virginal is nothing but this. In all
cases never confront the open air till you

have well dried, and lightly powdered, your face. Carrots, which are a specific for the complexion, are thought highly of as a remedy for freckles. Take a thin carrot soup for your early breakfast instead of *café au lait*, with rye bread steeped in it.

Warts.

I think it was Montaigne who said " I love Paris, down to its very warts." That may be all very well for a great and magnificent city, but a pretty or beautiful face is terribly disfigured by these little hard bumps, vulgarly called *poireaux*.

I will therefore give some safe and simple means of getting rid of them :—

1st. Take some small doses of sulphate of magnesia (Epsom salts). For an adult the dose is from 60 to 90 grains a day for a month. After a fortnight of this treatment the warts have almost always disappeared.

2nd. In other days the fuller's teazel (*Labrum Veneris* or *Virga Pastoris* or, scientifically, *Dipsacus Fullonum*) was much prized as a remedy for warts; it was thus named because the leaves are arranged in the form of a basin, "and in fact the said leaves, sometimes bent into a bow, represent a basin wherein water and dew will always be found." The warts were rubbed with the water or juice found in these hollows.

3rd. Someone recommends that the wart should be pressed against the bone with the thumb, moving it in and out till the roots become irritated and painful. The wart will then melt away or fall off.

4th. Warts may be cured by rubbing them three or four times a day with a potato. Cut the end off the potato, and rub the wart with the part freshly cut; and after each rubbing, cut another slice off the potato.

5th. Rub night and morning with the following ointment:—4 parts by weight of chromate of potassium, well mixed with

5 parts of axungia or vaseline. Three or four weeks of this treatment will effect a cure.

6th. Lemon-juice will remove warts. Touch them three or four times a day with a camel's-hair brush steeped in the juice.

7th. Take a slate, and have it calcined in the fire; then reduce it to powder, and mix this powder with strong vinegar. Rub the excrescences with this wash, and they will give way to the treatment.

8th. European heliotrope (herb for warts, or *Verrucaria* in the pharmacopœia) is much vaunted, and its juice, mixed with salt, is said to destroy warts and lumps.

9th. Caustic or nitrate of silver exterminates warts very well; they should be touched with it every two or three days.

10th. A wart may be got rid of by steeping it several times a day in castor-oil.

11th. Melt some spirit of salts in water, and wash the warts with this water. This caustic will make them fall off in scales.

D*

The utmost care must be taken, especially if this remedy is used for the face.

12th. The caustic juice of the greater celandine may also be used.

It is a mistake to imagine that warts can be caught by contact. Before burning a wart with caustic, it should be cut to the quick.

Diseases of the Skin affecting the Face.

For the little scurfy eruptions which sometimes come on the face, one doctor of my acquaintance recommends rubbing with lemon-juice—successfully.

Ulcerated eruptions have been cured by bathing with strawberry-juice. An easier or more agreeable remedy can hardly be imagined. It is much less repugnant than, and quite as efficacious as, a *live* yellow slug, with which the sore used to be rubbed till the unhappy mollusc was used up. Bathing with strawberries is sovereign against ulcers as well as eruptions. If used daily while they are in season, they will drive away all redness, inflammation, pimples, etc., from the face.

Eczema on the face should be treated with poultices of potato flour, and the patient should drink a tisane of alder-root ($\frac{1}{2}$ ounce to a quart of water, decocted). A pint of the decoction should be taken, fasting, at two or three different times; another pint to be taken in the evening, at least two hours after the last meal. The diet should be very severe — neither wine nor coffee, no game, fish, or pork in any shape. In this case strawberries are forbidden, as well as asparagus, cabbage, turnips, and cheese, with the exception of Gruyère.

Almost the same diet should be used for redness (*couperose*) of the face; and for this the following lotion and ointment are also recommended :—

Lotion—refined sulphur, 1 oz.; alcohol, $\frac{1}{2}$ oz.; distilled water, 1 pint. Sponge the face with this mixture often. (Hot vapour douches are also excellent.)

Ointment—1 part of oxide of zinc to 10 parts of vaseline. Anoint the face with this, going to bed. This treatment should be interrupted twice a week for twenty-four hours. Before bathing or anointing the face, it should be well washed in tepid water.

It is unnecessary to say that these simple remedies may be used for the same diseases on other parts of the body.

Depilatories.

Some women have another and still deeper cause for despair. I speak of the hairs which appear on the chin in maturity, and of the down which may darken and give a mannish look even to the rosy lips of a girl of twenty.

Let none give way to despair—there is more than one remedy for these ills :—

1st. I consider that the use of a pair of

small steel pincers is the most efficacious and unobjectionable of all remedies. But care must be taken to pull the hair out by the roots, and not to break it during the operation: it requires a determined pull. An electrical operation has lately been much vaunted also—it is called electrolysis; the hair never grows again after this operation, while the use of the pincers must be constantly renewed.

2nd. Water distilled from the leaves and root of celandine. It is applied as a compress on the desired spot, and left on all night. It should be repeated till the down disappears.

3rd. Sulpho-hydrate of soda 1½ drachms, of quick lime 5 drachms, starch 5 drachms. Mix these into a paste with a little water, and apply it, keeping it on for an hour, and washing with fresh water afterwards.

4th. Cut up an oak-apple into little pieces, and put it into a basin, with white wine over it to the depth of a finger. Let

it steep in this bath for twenty-four hours ;
then distil it with boiling water till nothing
more ascends. Apply it in a compress on
the affected part, and keep it on all night.
Repeat this every night till the desired
result is produced.

If it were true, as some people affirm,
that lentils have the property of increasing
in length and thickness the growth of the
hair, of causing the moustaches of youths
and the beards of men to grow and become
bushy, then indeed should women who
have a tendency to down on their lips and
chins eschew having anything to do with
this formidable vegetable.

Waters and Cosmetics for the Face.

Never use any kind of paint; all rouges
are bad for the skin, and white paints are
dangerous.

The Chinese have, however, discovered an
inoffensive rouge, made of the juice of beet-
root, with which they redden their cheeks.

The ordinary essences, ointments, and powders of commerce, are either without any effect at all, or produce exactly the opposite to the one hoped for.

Nevertheless I shall give the recipes for some waters and cosmetics, but it is because I am certain of their perfect harmlessness, and that some of them are refreshing to the skin.

We begin with the simplest.

Very greasy and oily skins will be the better for being washed with wine (all those of France and the Rhine) about once a fortnight. If the skin is dark, red wine should be preferred. Fresh cucumber-juice is among the best things for the skin; and almost equally good is the water in which spinach in flower has been boiled. But strawberry-juice—of which we have already spoken—is superior to both.

In the sixteenth century the water in which beans were cooked was in great favour, and this mealy water did really deserve the reputation it then had.

The Gauls, whose brilliant carnation was the envy of the Roman patricians, washed their faces with the froth of beer. They also used chalk dissolved in vinegar. I do not know what to think of this solution, but I can answer for it that the foam of beer is still used with advantage by the women of the North. *Belladonna* takes its name from the use the Italians made of its juice for improving the complexion.

The Roman ladies of antiquity, who were such great coquettes, considered, it is said, the blood of the hare as the most precious of cosmetics—a somewhat repellent recipe for modern taste.

The following lotion is excellent:—A wineglassful of fresh lemon-juice, a pint of rain-water, five drops of rose-water. This should be kept well corked, and used from *time to time* it will preserve the colour of the skin.

Flabby and relaxed skins will derive benefit from the following cosmetics, used

at intervals of eight days :—Equal parts of
milk, and brandy made from corn. Wet
the face with this mixture by means of a
soft towel, after having washed, and before
getting into bed. The result is not immediate, but after a year the skin will have
become sufficiently strung up, firm, smooth,
and fine.

If you have a very dry skin, and require
oily ointment, instead of the softening
creams so erroneously praised, use highly-
rectified vaseline, with a few drops of
perfumed oil in it.

Oil of cacao enriches a dry skin. A
mixture called "Princess of Wales" consists of half a pint of milk, with the juice of
a slice of Portugal lemon squeezed into it.
The face is to be anointed with this mixture
at bedtime, and washed with fresh (not cold)
water the next morning.

Lastly, here are some real cosmetics
which are not dangerous to the tissues:—At
the end of May take a pound of the freshest

butter possible (of course, perfectly unmixed
with salt or anything else); place it in a
white basin, and put it where the sun will
be on it the whole day, but where no dust
or dirt can fall on it. When the butter is
melted, pour over it plantain-juice, and mix
the two well together with a wooden spoon.
Allow the sun to absorb the plantain-water,
and put more juice on six times a day.
Continue this till the butter has become
as white as snow. During the last few
days add a little orange-flower and rose
water. Anoint your face with this ointment
at night, and wipe it carefully in the
morning. This is an old and good recipe
of the time of *la belle Gabrielle*.

Here is one that dates from the time of
the Crusades:—Boil six fresh eggs hard,
take out the yolks, and replace them by
myrrh and powdered sugar-candy in equal
parts. Then join the two halves of the
white of the eggs (which had been cut in
two to take out the yolks), and expose the

six eggs to the fire on a plate. A liquid will come from them which is to be mixed with an ounce of lard or white vaseline, prepared as I shall direct under the heading "Pomades and Hair-Oils." The face should be covered in the morning with the oint-ment thus obtained, which should be allowed to dry on it, and then gently wiped off.

It is said that this secret of beauty was brought back from Palestine by a *beau chevalier* with whom a sultana had fallen in love. If his lady-love got wind of his infidelity, she may well have forgiven it for the sake of this cosmetic which he brought back from the harem into which he had intruded.

Cosmetics for the Hands, Arms, etc.

The recipes which we have given above may be used for the neck, arms, and hands.

Here is another, to be used on evenings, when the arms and neck are uncovered :—
80 grains of oxide of zinc to 1 oz. of

glycerine, with the addition of a little rose-
water.   This preparation has the advantage
of not coming off on the coats of one's
partners.

The Use of Face Powder.

I have said that it is sometimes
necessary to powder the face, and I have
pointed out on what occasions.   But it
must be done artistically and with a light
hand—simply enough to give the skin the
delightful surface of the peach.

Nothing is so ugly as a face powdered
like a Pierrot ready to grin.   The spectator
should be left in doubt as to whether the
skin is imperceptibly veiled by a thin cloud
of powder, or whether it is the natural
bloom.   Then the effect is pretty, especially
under a veil; not but that a natural skin is
preferable if it is fine, smooth, and just the
right colour.

The puff should be dipped into the
powder with precaution, so as not to come

out too full of powder, which will prevent a wise use of it. Nor should the puff be wiped on the skin; it should barely touch the face, and that in a succession of small quick taps. Care must be taken not to powder the eyebrows and eyelashes, and to take off any that may have adhered to the lips.

A touch of powder should be put on the whole of the face, except the eyes, eyebrows, and lips; otherwise any part that is not touched with powder will look ridiculously dark compared with those that are.

THE HAIR.

Fair and Dark Women—Blondes and Brunettes.

Is there a woman living who has not coveted the " mantle of a king " sung by Musset?

> " Cette chevelure qui l'inonde,
> Plus longue qu'un manteau de roi."

And in truth it is a splendid ornament that
Nature has bestowed on her chosen ones,
and which they ought to know how to
preserve—as, indeed, everyone ought, no
matter what kind of hair they have been
given.

Of course, to be really beautiful, hair
should be abundant, fine, and brilliant. But
let not those despair altogether whose hair
is thin, short, coarse, or lustreless; these
faults may be somewhat, if not a great deal,
diminished by intelligent efforts.

All the beautiful qualities we have
enumerated will not suffice for many women
if their hair is black as a raven's wing.
They want to be fair, as all, or nearly all,
the fatal and fascinating women of history
have been.

Eve, they say, was fair as honey; the
locks of Venus streamed over her divine
shoulders in a golden flood; the hair of
Ceres was the colour of the harvest; Helen
the beautiful, whom even the old men of

Troy could not see without emotion, crowned her adorable head with fair hair like ripe corn; Salome, who asked for and obtained the head of John the Baptist, had yellow hair—at least, the old masters painted her fair, like the young Jewesses of high birth; Lucretia Borgia, Lady Macbeth the murderess, and Queen Mary were all blondes; Queen Elizabeth had red hair; and Catherine and Marie de Medicis were also fair.

Cousin thus describes the hair of his adored Duchesse de Longueville: "Her tresses were of a *blond cendré* and of the utmost fineness. They descended in abundant curls, inundating her admirable shoulders, and ornamenting the delicate oval of her face."

Anne of Austria, again, was a blonde; so was Madame de Sevigné, whose way of dressing her hair is still famous; and the gentle La Vallière was also fair.

The fair hair of Marie Antoinette and

of Madame de Lamballe would have been
enough to make them beautiful. Madame
Emile de Girardin also had a remarkable
head of fair hair; and one of the beauties
of the Empress Eugénie was her very
blonde hair.

I confess I admire this fair hair—
whether *cendré*, golden, or auburn—and
this taste has been shared from antiquity.
In the time of Pericles the Greeks washed
their hair in soap-suds and water to take
out the colour, afterwards rubbing it with
the fat of goats, beech-ashes, and yellow
flowers. Then they let it hang over
their shoulders to dry. The Germans were
proud of their light hair, and those who
had it not by nature had recourse to art to
help them. Washing the hair with beer
was supposed to be efficacious for making
it fair, and also an application of lime.
Roman ladies cursed their sombre-coloured
hair, and Ovid relates that they covered
their heads with blonde wigs bought in

Germania at high prices. Everyone knows
what pains and trouble the Venetian
women took in order to attain that flame-
coloured copper-tint for their hair which is
called the *blond Titien*.

Nowadays there are some who get their
hair dyed mahogany colour in the most
scientific and approved manner ; it is
perfectly hideous. Others who are blondes
by nature make the colour of their hair
still fairer with the help of oxidised water.
Englishwomen wash their hair with rum
and an infusion of colocynth, to prevent it
from becoming browner with advancing
years.

It seems that in olden days (those
happy olden days !) there were many more
blondes than there are now. Do you wish
to know why, even in northern countries,
the hair becomes darker century after
century ? " Heaven," says a humorist,
"sent a great many golden-haired women
on the earth to charm the other half of

humanity. Seeing this, the devil, who hates man, sent us cooks : they with their sauces and ragouts have disordered the human hair, and these disorders manifest themselves outwardly by the sombre colour of the hair." Some grain of truth may perhaps lie hidden under this absurdity.

Arab women and the subjects of the Shah prefer dark hair, and they dye their beautiful black hair darker with henna. The leaves of this plant, reduced to powder and mixed with water, form a cosmetic with which the hair is carefully covered. This paste is taken off some hours after, by washing with water tinged with indigo, which leaves the hair a splendid colour for some days afterwards.

The Russians admire nut-brown hair above all others, affirming that Christ had hair of that colour.

Auburn or light chestnut hair is much thought of in England ; it suits the fresh faces of the daughters of Albion.

How to Dress the Hair.

In spite of my avowed preference for fair hair, I would advise no one to change the colour of their hair, were it as dark or black as Erebus. Nature gives to each face the frame which is most becoming to it, and it is impossible to improve or correct her on this point.

To make the best of whatever hair we possess is to choose the best way of dressing it. But it is curious that in arranging their style of hair-dressing, women never consider either the colour or the texture of their hair.

We should not try to curl smooth hair, any more than we should flatten down curly or even wavy hair. It is certain that some faces require the frame which their naturally fuzzy and curly hair gives them. Black hair and the faces it goes with are not improved by being frizzed; they need smooth *bandeaux*; long lustrous curls, large plaits. Red hair should be frizzed; when fuzzed out and separated, the colour becomes softened. Heavy tresses of brown hair are very pretty. Blonde hair will bear almost every style of dressing : it is charming in smooth polished bands, adorable in a halo round the forehead.

Why do not women dress their hair to suit the particular character of their own faces, instead of making themselves ugly by following whatever is the fashion? Women ought even to have the courage to allow their hair to become white. All dyes founded on silver or lead are dangerous. Moreover, they only make the hair and complexion ugly. Let us accept the snows the years bring; they harmonise with the countenance which time and suffering have given us—and framed in white hair, certain faces become strangely softened and improved. There is both grace and dignity in disdaining to repair the irreparable ravages of time. " And what about powder? " I shall be asked. I would not

powder even white hair. Powdered hair
makes the features look hard, as does everything that is not natural. The refined
faces of the eighteenth century would have
been even more charming if Richelieu had
not thought of concealing his first silver
threads with flour. Moreover, as there is
nothing new under the sun, the conqueror
of Port Mahon has not even the credit of
inventing powdered hair. The ancient
Greeks, who sometimes dyed their hair
white, had the custom, too, of powdering it,
so as to render it the azure colour of the
skies and waves; or by means of coloured
powders to give it the changing tints of a
pigeon's throat, or that of the honey of
Mount Hymettus.

If the hair is drawn too tight, plastered
down, or too much twisted, it is no longer
an ornament, and looks as if the owner was
anxious to get rid of it, instead of treating
it as an embellishment. Indeed, the effect
is disastrous. A certain amount of freedom

and *abandon* should be allowed to the hair; and this is also good for the hair itself.

Very deep thick fringes coming down low on the forehead give an animal look to the face; but a few small light little curls on the top of the forehead are very becoming.

To dispose the hair becomingly, the feature and structure of the figure should be considered. A small thin woman looks ridiculous if she enlarges her head too much by the way she wears her hair. If the forehead is high and prominent, and the features large, dragging the hair up *à la Chinoise* will be simply hideous. If you make your parting a very little to one side of the head, it will take five years off your age; but a parting quite at the side will make the most delicately moulded face appear masculine. Everyone should avoid an eccentric *coiffure;* and the size of the head should never be increased by a mass of false hair. The head will have more refinement and distinction if left its natural shape, and will be more in harmony with the figure to which it belongs.

A worn and elderly-looking woman will find herself wonderfully improved by covering her hair, even if it is still plentiful, with a lace mantilla, which will veil the ravages of time about her face, and will form a graceful frame for it. An old woman looks frightful with a bare head; and the light shadows thrown by lace will do much to dissimulate the effects of age.

How to Take Care of the Hair.

The fashion of frizzing the hair, whether with hot irons, pins, or any other artificial means of making it wavy, is, it must be confessed, a disastrous one for the beauty and growth of the hair. And what would become of us, with these short hairs round the forehead that have become crisp, stiff, and coarse by frequent cutting and curling, if the decree went forth that the fashion for smooth bands should come in?

I know that many women, thinking themselves very clever, wear a false fringe. But this opens up new danger. Very often false hair, in spite of the purifying it has undergone, has communicated skin disease to the wearer. Hair cut from the heads of the Chinese is specially apt to spread this infection. Fortunately, the hair of the Celestials is easily discerned; very coarse, harsh, black, and brilliant, is this hair that comes from the extreme East.

False hair should be often renewed. If it is cut off the head of a living person it keeps its vitality for about two years, or a little longer. After that it becomes unequal, stiff, and rough, and can no longer be used. Hair taken from the dead is never used by hairdressers who value their reputation. It cannot be frizzed or curled without great difficulty.

As few hair-pins as possible should be

used for confining the hair, so as not to irritate the skin of the head, as they often do. I am speaking of black japanned hair-pins. Those made of tortoise-shell (either real or imitation) and the thick-gilt wire hair-pins have not this drawback, for they cannot make painful pricks.

It is well sometimes to change the way of dressing the hair for a day or two ; it makes the hair grow thin if it is always done exactly in the same manner, and is always twisted in the same direction.

If the hair is parted, it should be done afresh every day. This daily operation keeps the parting very narrow and close, and the contrary happens if this trifling trouble is neglected.

It is further necessary to cut about an inch off the ends of the hair at the new moon during the first quarter. The hair will gain as much from one new moon to another ; there is no fear, therefore, of diminishing its length. At the end of the

E

year it will be found to be the same as at
the beginning; and some hair will even
grow much longer, thanks to this habit of
pointing it. I do not believe that the
tranquil queen of the night has really much
to do with the growth of the hair; but
who knows?—for, after all, there are occult
and mysterious influences which science has
not yet explained. It is doubtless to the
regularity of the proceeding that the good
effects are to be attributed. One thing is
certain—that hair which has the ends cut
at every new moon will grow more
abundantly.

It is best to sleep with the head uncovered. Hair that is left free at night
will be finer, more silky, and neater than if
it is imprisoned in a cap. But one must be
used from childhood to sleep with nothing
on the head. In this case the hair should
be raised above the ears, without pulling it,
and loosely plaited in one large plait, tied
with a ribbon, and not fastened in any other

way. Beware of plaiting the hair under a
cap or net; the more free and separated it
is, the more shining and lustrous it will
become. Above all, let no one wear such a
thing as a starched cap; the starch is sure
to get among the hair, and to spoil it.

Those who have been used from childhood to wearing night-caps will be likely to
catch colds, toothache, or earache, if they
change this habit, especially in winter.
And even those who have never had the
habit will do well to adopt a night-cap in
old age.

To keep the hair nice, it should be
brushed on going to bed at night, as well as
when dressing in the daytime, with a soft
brush. The best brushes are those with
short bristles, and unbleached. The hair
should be disentangled from the extreme
end, after having divided it into as many
tresses as necessary. If you begin to comb
from the roots to the ends, without having
separated the hair into three or four parts,

you will do a great deal of damage. You
will certainly break it, and make it ugly and
impossible to give it a cared-for aspect. It
is very good to burnish the hair with
the hand. In Turkey the slave who has
charge of the sultana's hair caresses and
rolls it about in her hands until it is as
supple, soft, and brilliant as a skein of silk.

It is as well to use as little grease, oils,
or pomades as possible.

The Roman ladies thought that walnut-
juice made the hair luxuriant.

How to Clean the Hair.

The frequent use of a fine toothcomb is
fatal for the hair, especially when it is
falling out. Nevertheless it is necessary to
keep the hair and the scalp clean.

One of my friends, who has the prettiest
hair in the world—soft, neat, wavy, and
burnished—cleans it from time to time with
a mineral essence.

The Chinese, who have good hair,

although stiff and coarse, use a mixture of honey and flowers.

English people use the following solution:—A teacupful of salt in a quart of rain-water. This can be used after it has stood for twelve hours. To one cup of the preparation add a cup of warm rain-water. Wash the hair well with this, rinsing and rubbing it, as well as the scalp, with a towel till they are quite dry.

Italians, who are blessed with very vigorous heads of hair, wash it and the scalp with a decoction made from the roots of nettles.

The Creoles of Cuba make a decoction from rosemary leaves, which they consider cleans, strengthens, and sóftens the hair.

An excellent lotion is made as follows: —Boil 1¾ oz. of roots of soap-wort in a pint and a half of water. The preparation should be used warm, and the hair and head must be dried quickly with warm towels.

The yolk of an egg is very good for

cleaning the hair, and helps to make it grow. The skin of the head should be well rubbed with the yolk, and then rinsed with warm water. The white of eggs, well beaten up into a froth, is also one of the simplest and best preparations ; it should be used in the same way as the yolks.

Here, finally, are some more elaborate lotions for those who disdain simple remedies :—

1st. One that is useful for washing the hair, besides being good when it is falling out, and for headaches :—Take half a pint of rectified and sweet-smelling spirit, dissolve in it 8 grains of sulphate of quinine, and leave it to infuse for two days in a bottle hermetically corked. After that time, add a pint of old rum and 1¾ ounces of yellow quinine in powder. Leave these together for three days ; then rinse the sediment with about two-fifths of water, and mix the two liquids, filtering them through paper.

2nd. A chemist gives this recipe to

enable one to make a quinine wash oneself for washing the head :—Sulphate of quinine 46 grains, enough *eau de Rahel* to dissolve it; opoponax 5 drams, dissolved in the necessary quantity of rectified alcohol at 96°; add 3 drops of patchouly, 2½ drachms of essence of violets, and 2½ drachms of essence of bouquet. Make it up to six quarts by adding enough alcohol at 40°. Throw into the liquid 2½ ounces of powdered orris-root; leave it to stand for eight days, and then strain it.

3rd. Shampooing mixture used in England :—A quart of hot or cold water, in which 1 ounce of carbonate of soda has been dissolved and half an ounce of Pears' soap cut into small pieces. Add to this some drops of perfumed essence and 1 ounce of spirits of wine. After washing the hair with this preparation, it should be rinsed with tepid water, and then both the head and hair should be rubbed with warm towels till they are dry.

It is always well to dry the hair rapidly and thoroughly; and after drying, it should be allowed to hang loosely over the shoulders for an hour or two. The hair will get much less matted if after shaking it out it is allowed to hang loose over the shoulders while one is dressing and undressing.

White hair (and, indeed, some other hair) can be admirably cleaned with flour; it, as well as the skin of the head, should be rubbed with the flour, and then carefully brushed. I think this is perhaps the best way of all. It is a pity that it is difficult to use it with dark hair, for obvious reasons.

Diseases of the Hair.

Dandruff is not only very unsightly, but brings baldness in its train. This affection may be obstinate, as it is often due to a bad state of health; but before having recourse to medical treatment simple remedies like the following can be tried:—

1st. Melt 2 ounces of crystals of soda

in a quart of water, and 1 ounce of eau de Cologne. Dip a hairbrush into this water, and pass it over the affected parts several times a day.

2nd. Apply lemon-juice to the scalp; the juice should touch the hair as little as possible.

3rd. Take 2½ drachms of Panama wood, and boil it in a pint of rain-water. With the decoction wash the parts affected two or three times a week.

When the hair falls out without reason, there must be some disease; and the same may be said when it splits at the points. Grief causes the hair to fall out and get thin. There is no remedy for this but time and forgetfulness and happier days.

Often the hair falls out without any apparent cause; when it does, be sure you are out of health, perhaps without knowing it yourself—especially if your hair becomes dead and rough. We know that an animal is in good health when its fur is silky and bright.

E *

With all due respect it is just the same
with men and even women. Watch yourself in this case, and find out what the
mischief is. Under such circumstances a
good treatment for the hair is to soap the
scalp and then anoint it, rubbing in well a
mixture of castor-oil, oil of sweet almonds,
and of tannin.

A girl of fifteen may suddenly find her
beautiful hair falling out without any ap-
preciable cause. It should then be cut
off to about the lobe of the ear, and a
stimulating lotion applied to the scalp.
There is no need for anxiety, unless the
hair does not begin to grow again. A
doctor would advise in that case that the
head should be shaved, and washed three
times a week with the following preparation :
—Half an ounce of colocynth in a pint of
good Jamaica rum. This should be strained
at the end of three days, and the infusion
poured into a bottle and well corked. The
head should be vigorously brushed before

the application. The hair will grow again,
and it will be supposed that it is the colocynth that has changed its former tint to a
charming golden one.

Baldness.

A man may put up with being bald, for
he has so many fellow-sufferers; moreover,
a man's face is not much the worse for this
defect. But a bald woman is indeed to be
pitied. She cannot accept this misfortune—
at least, she must hide it by every conceiv-
able means. She must take refuge in a
wig, or in wearing before her time lace caps
or mantillas in the house, which always ages
the wearer a little.

Nevertheless, the number of bald women
increases every day. This state of things
is attributed to the curling-irons, which
have been too much used; to the wigs; to
the false hair, which has caused the real to
fall out; to the woollen *fichus* thrown over
the head to keep it from the cold either in

the house or garden; to the velvet bows worn on the top of the head; etc. etc. There is very likely some truth in all this; but in my opinion it is to the dyes, above all, that the evil is due.

People do not wait now for their hair to turn white before they dye it; they vary the colour of their hair with their toilette. One day they appear blonde, the next red or brown. Those who have black hair get it dyed an indelible mahogany tint. When women with fair hair see it getting darker, they immediately try to make it light again with oxidised water, which spoils the texture of the hair.

Those who find their hair turning white would go to the Prince of Darkness himself to conceal the snows of time, and one soon perceives that they have used infernal measures. This is a sad want of common-sense. We must remain what we are, or what we have become. It is high time to remedy the evil for the sake of future

generations. We must go back to simple
hair-dressing, without the addition of false
hair or crimping-irons. People will take
care to cover their heads with silk and not
woollen kerchiefs; velvet will be given up
as an ornament for the hair; and, above
all, dyes will be renounced. The natural
colour of the hair will be kept; it will be
allowed to darken, and then to grow white;
and grey hair itself will not be powdered.
At this cost the hair will remain abundant
and vigorous, even in those of advanced age,
and will allow of being prettily and gracefully dressed.

Are not thick *bandeaux*, even at the
pepper-and-salt stage, preferable to a bald
head or to false hair, which it is easily
seen does not belong to the head it
is on?

There is but one way of remedying
feminine baldness, and that is by inventing
pretty lace caps to hide it; and mothers
who are thus afflicted should teach their

daughters how to avoid the necessity for this addition to their toilette.

Recipes for Preventing the Hair from Falling Out.

Brunettes may stop their raven locks from falling out by the application of lemon-juice to their scalps.

Another remedy for the same evil is the following :—Wash the head every night with this mixture, rubbing it in hard : A teaspoonful of salt and one scruple of quinine, added to a pint of ordinary brandy; shake the mixture well. The following recipe I have seen made, and have known good results from its use :—Three common onions cleaned and put into a quart of rum for twenty-four hours ; the onions are then taken out, and the rum used to rub the scalp with every other day. The slight odour of onions it may retain evaporates in a few minutes.

The *Lancet* recommends the following

pomade for hair falling out:—5 parts of
tincture of jaborandi, 3 parts of lanoline,
20 parts of glycerine; mixed with the
help of a little soft-soap; the head to be
rubbed every night with a *little* of this
pomade on the end of your finger.

A friend of mine derived benefit from a
decoction of the leaves of the walnut in
water, with which he wetted the scalp every
night by means of a sponge. He had been
obliged to give up the use of a fine comb,
and the following had been ordered for
use in dressing his hair in the morning:
—Unguent of balsam 30 parts, tannin
1 part, tincture of benzoin 3 parts. Again,
a man who was having pilocarpine injected
for his sight recovered all his hair, at the
age of sixty.

The head should not be shaved after an
illness. The hair will at once stop falling out if it is cut three times (I am, of
course, speaking of women's hair). Each
time a certain length should be taken off in

proportion to the length of the hair; the
third time it should be left longer than to the
lobe of the ear.   One must resign oneself to
wearing the hair like a boy at first, then
like a little girl as it grows longer.   The
most grievous results might ensue from
wearing a wig or false hair of any kind, for
one would risk losing what remained of
one's hair without hope of recovery.   From
the day on which the hair is begun to be
cut, the head should be rubbed with an
infusion of quinine and a mixture of rum
and castor-oil in equal parts.

Tepid sage-tea is also recommended on
condition that the head is well dried with
warm towels.

Pomades and Hair-Oils.

Some hair is so dry that it cannot
do without pomade for fear of breaking it.
A doctor recommends oil of vaseline very
much rectified (liquid vaseline), and perfumed according to taste.

If other oils or pomades are preferred,
they should be prepared at home, for bad
pomades cause or hasten the loss of hair.
Care should be taken above all to clarify
the grease or oil used, and for this it must
undergo a preliminary preparation. The
oils or marrows should be put into a *bain-
marie* with 3 parts of powdered benzoin, and
3 parts of powdered balm of Tolu to every
100 parts of the grease. It must be
stirred often with a wooden spoon. After
two hours' boiling, the oils and grease are
strained through a cloth. The benzoin acid,
like vanilla, possesses the property of preventing fatty substances with which it is in-
corporated becoming rancid. Vaseline never
becomes rancid. To make another pomade,
take 3 ounces of the grease prepared in the
best manner, 2 ounces of beef marrow, and
1 ounce of sweet-almond oil; before these
substances are quite stiff and cold, perfume
them with 30 minims of essence of bergamot
and 1 drachm of essence of violet.

Some people use water instead of pomade ; nothing is worse for the hair. The habit of using the saliva to smooth the hair is a disgusting and often a dangerous one.

How to Clean Combs and Brushes.

There is nothing better than ammonia for cleaning hair-brushes ; it does not soften the bristles as soap and soda do. Put a teaspoonful of ammonia in a quart of water; dip the brush into this, preserving the ivory or wooden backs as well as possible. An immersion of a few seconds will suffice to take out all the grease. The brush should then be dipped in clear water and dried in the open air, but *not* in the sun.

Combs must never be washed. They can be cleaned with a tightly-stretched string or with a card, by sticking the teeth into cotton-wool, or by using a little flat hard brush, or any of the implements invented by hairdressers for the purpose. There are special brushes for brushing out the combs every time they are used.

The greatest neatness is necessary for all implements used for hair-dressing.

Ammonia and the Hair.

Ammonia takes the colour out of the hair. Beware, therefore, if you use it in your bath, not to wet your hair. Indeed, the hair should be kept from all contact with water, except what is actually necessary for cleansing purposes.

THE MOUTH.

The Breath.

THE purity of the breath has a great effect on the beauty and preservation of the teeth; and, moreover, if that purity is altered, one's fellow-creatures withdraw more or less to a distance from one. It is obvious, therefore, that the freshness of the breath is of the greatest importance, and that we must not disdain the means by which it may be preserved, or restored if lost.

Sobriety, health, complete abstinence from strong flavours (such as garlic and onions), and clean and healthy teeth : these are the conditions, in a word, which will admit of our preserving to old age, and even till death, a breath as sweet and fresh as a child's.

Diseases of the mouth and stomach, neglected and decayed teeth, the abuse of alcoholic liquors, too high living, rich and spiced dishes, are all compromising to the breath. If the cause should arise from the stomach, from the teeth, or from a disease of the mouth, the use of purgating mineral waters, powdered chalk, or magnesia and bicarbonate of soda, are all indicated.

Bad teeth should be extracted relentlessly. If it is impossible to go at once to the dentist, small pieces of iris-root should be kept in the mouth to counteract the effect of the bad state of the teeth.

The people of Java eat the bark of cinnamon to perfume their mouths and make them sweet. The famous little dancers of Kampong, at the Paris Exhibition, had brought a large provision of it.

The resinous substance which flows from an incision made in the bark of a gum-tree is an astringent for the gums, and gives a delicious odour to the breath. It is gum in tears; the sultanas make much use of it.

If we are to believe Martial, the Roman ladies used tooth-picks cut out of the wood of the turpentine-tree.

A mixture of tincture of camphor and myrrh is excellent for gargling and washing out the mouth when any accident of health affects the breath temporarily : a few drops of each in a glass of water. If myrrh alone is used, ten drops will suffice.

When you have eaten *côlelettes à la*

soubise, or any other dish in which there is onion, swallow a cup of black coffee immediately after. Coffee is an antidote to the atrocious odour which that bulb communicates to the respiratory organs. As for garlic, let no one ever touch it.

I have heard of a very easy and practicable remedy for the unpleasant evil of which we are speaking, namely :—

Powdered charcoal	1 part.
„ white sugar	1 part.
„ good chocolate	3 parts.

Melt the chocolate in a *bain-marie,* then add the sugar and charcoal; mix them all very well together. After the preparation has been allowed to get cold on marble, cut it up into small squares, and eat three or four of these during the day.

The Lips.

I should hardly be forgiven if I left the subject of the mouth without mentioning the lips.

To be beautiful, the lips should have the red of raspberries, and they should be soft, and not chapped. Red lips are incompatible with certain temperaments. In such cases people must resign themselves to pale-coloured lips, for all attempts to heighten their colour will only succeed for the moment, and be detrimental to the softness and the suppleness of the tissues.

Do not have recourse, therefore, to friction with alcohol, vinegars, or cosmetics; you will certainly lose more in the long run than you gain temporarily. If your lips are not rough, they will always have a certain freshness and smoothness, which in itself is a charm, in spite of a pale pink colour. Alcohol, vinegars, and rouge will destroy the exquisite delicacy of the epidermis, so essential to this feature. How often do children say to women who kiss them, " Your lips prick," because they have made their skin harsh by using stupid remedies. Many women bite their lips on entering a room, to make them red. But, besides the fact that the colour thus obtained only lasts a few seconds, the habit of biting the lips makes them sore and inclined to chap.

If your lips are naturally dry and rough, rub them a little every night with equal parts of water and glycerine.

Do not pass your tongue over your lips; for, besides being against the rules of polite society, the dampness thus produced is not good for them.

If pimples from feverishness come and disfigure your lips, touch them lightly with powdered alum, and they will soon be cured.

Extravagant laughter on all occasions, for everything and nothing, must not be indulged in by those who wish to keep their lips pretty. Avoid contortions of the mouth in speaking — does not everyone know people who draw in and push out their lips when they speak? Beware of tricks: I knew a dressmaker who stuck out her lips every time she drew out her needle. It is easy to understand that excessive laughter, contortions of the face, and tricks, will disfigure the mouth and bring on premature old age, while many matrons remain pretty from knowing how to preserve the freshness of their lips and the charm of their smile.

To reduce lips that are too thick, rubbing with tannin may be tried.

Pomades for the Lips.

One of the small and disfiguring ills of life—chapped lips—may be easily cured.

Here are some prescriptions which are very good in this case :—

(1) Pure wax ... ... 2 parts
    Olive oil ... ... 11 ,,

Melt the wax over a gentle fire, and add the oil, mixing them well together. Perfume it with a few drops of tincture of benzoin, and allow it to get cold.

(2) White wax, oil of sweet almonds, essence of rose, and a little carmine.

(3) *Pommade à la Sultane :—*

White wax	1 drachm.
Spermaceti	1 ,,
Balsam of Peru	1 ,,
Sweet-almond oil	6¼ ounces.
Rose-water	10 drachms

Dissolve the wax and spermaceti in oil *au bain-marie ;* pour them into a marble mortar warmed with boiling water; heat vigorously, then add by degrees the rose-water and the balsam, still stirring quickly, till they are completely mixed and the water is all absorbed.

(4) Oil of sweet almonds	15 drachms.
White wax	6 ,,
Butter of cacao	2 ,,
Spermaceti	2 ,,
Orchanet	4 ,,

Amalgamate these ingredients well over a gentle fire *au bain-marie ;* strain through muslin, and perfume with attar of roses.

These pomades should be put into very small pots, and carefully covered or corked.

The Teeth, and How to Keep Them Clean.

Théophile Gautier speaks somewhere of " a dazzling smile of pearls."

It is certain that nothing increases the charm of a smile so much, and nothing is so necessary to it, as a double row of perfectly good white teeth, disclosed when the lips open to smile.

Pretty teeth are a *sine quâ non* to beauty. Good teeth—which are almost always pretty —are indispensable to health. " No teeth, no health," is a strictly true aphorism formulated by Professor Préterre, a surgeon-dentist who is justly celebrated in France and elsewhere.

The premature loss of the teeth brings on old age before its time. It is possible, I know, to restore to the mouth the "*mobilier*" it has lost (as they said in the eighteenth century), but at the cost of what endless worries to our persons is this reparation made !

It is better to guard jealously what nature has given us. Let us take care of our teeth, then, so as not to be disfigured by their loss, so as to escape destructive diseases, and the terrible sufferings caused by teeth that have been spoilt, and also to preserve the purity of the breath, which is a charm above many others.

Cleaning the teeth is the surest way of combating the causes of their ruin. They should be cleaned by careful brushing, both night and morning; and it is an excellent thing to rinse out the mouth after every meal that one takes at home. Particles of food which stick between the teeth decompose, and bring by degrees the horrible decay so fatal to the teeth and to the freshness of the breath.

Some people use cold water for cleaning their teeth and rinsing the mouth; I advise the use of tepid water always for both purposes. A slight infusion of mint may be used for cleaning the teeth, or the following mixture:—

1½ drachms of borax and 4½ drachms of pure glycerine in a quart of luke-warm water. The first prescription, however, is the simpler, and may suffice.

The tooth-brush should be small and nearly round, so as to get into every corner of the mouth. I shall further speak of those dentifrices and tooth powders which seem to me free from dangerous ingredients; for the majority of things of this sort, and those most advertised, only increase destruction of the teeth. There are, however, some that are efficacious, and of these I shall give the recipes.

It may be enough to use soap for the teeth three or four times a week (besides the usual brushing twice a day). For this, very pure white soap, such as Marseilles soap, should be used. At first the operation seems, I admit, very disagreeable; but one very soon gets used to it, and it is followed with happy results. Soap is an alkaline preparation, and alkalines are much recommended for the teeth ; it is an antiseptic, and every mouth requires, more or less, an antiseptic. Lastly, it removes the tartar which covers the teeth, which the most celebrated tooth-powder can only do by damaging the enamel to some extent.

Some people simply use salt, and with great advantage to themselves ; they rub the teeth with it, brushing and rinsing the mouth afterwards with tepid water. These people have very white teeth, and their gums are firm and red. Still, I should be afraid that this treatment would not suit everyone, while the soap may be adopted without fear, no matter what the teeth or the temperament may be.

The teeth should not be brushed length-ways. If this is done, the points of the gums will be injured and the teeth loosened. The upper teeth should be brushed from the top downwards (from the gums to the ends of the teeth), the lower teeth from the bottom upwards, also from the gums to the extremity of the teeth. The inside of the teeth should be brushed in the same fashion, and as carefully as the outside.

The Gums.

The gums must be taken care of, for when they are in a good state the teeth are likely to be the same.

When the gums are soft, here is a powder that will make them firm :—

Quinine	... ...	...	15 drachms.
Ratanhia in powder		...	6 ,,
Chlorate of potassium		...	5 ,,

These powders should be well mixed together so as to form but one, with which the gums are to be rubbed three or four times a day.

By degrees the gums should be accustomed to a more energetic friction. If they are very soft and bleed easily, they should be strengthened by often chewing cress or scurvy-grass (*cochlearia*), or by washing them with an infusion of gentian or of bramble-leaves, in which a few drops of quinine or *eau de Cologne* should be mixed.

Lemon also has a very good action on tender or even ulcerated gums. Dip a camel's-hair brush into the lemon-juice and tap the affected parts with it, without touching the teeth. Equal parts of tincture of ratanhia and tincture of Spanish camomile used in the same manner is much to be recommended. It should be done at night.

Another mixture with which the gums may be touched daily is the following :—

Tincture of cochlearia ...	...	50 grains.
Hydrate of chloral ...	...	5 ,,

But this is a strong remedy, and should not be used without medical advice.

A decoction of myrrh, tannin, and oak-bark would be an excellent wash for tender gums, as it acts as an astringent.

Some foods, such as sugar, bonbons, and confectionery, are bad for the teeth. It is said that dates and radishes, because they are acid, are also bad for the teeth. Too much acid destroys the enamel of the teeth. Figs, like sugar, weaken the teeth, and oils and greasy substances do them no good.

Beware of drinking immediately after taking hot soup, unless what you drink is lukewarm. If it is cold or iced, the teeth will suffer from this sudden change from a burning hot to a polar temperature. You should breathe through the nose, especially in cold weather (indeed, it is well to keep to this habit in summer also, for the health of the lungs). If you breathe through the mouth in winter, you expose your teeth to a current of air of a much lower temperature than that of your body. From this come inflammations of the periosteum and of the teeth themselves, and congestions of the mucous membrane, with acid secretions— but I must not become too scientific. All sensible people will understand that it is bad for the teeth to breathe through the

.F

mouth or to sleep with the mouth open, which generally happens when one lies on one's back. It is dangerous to pick the teeth, or even to touch them, with pins or any other metallic substances.

"When you eat," says an ancient author, "eat with both sides, so that one may relieve the other."

Toothache.

When you suffer from toothache, mistrust the ordinary remedies that are recommended. Creosote, cloves, essence of cinnamon, etc. etc., may perhaps ease your pain, but they will destroy your teeth. Go at once to the dentist; and if you are obliged to delay doing so, use only such remedies as are evidently harmless. For example, roll some parsley with a little salt up into a small ball, and put it into the ear on the side where the pain is. Or, again, paint the cheek with lemon-juice, or apply a hot flannel to the face. A scanty diet and

warm baths will sometimes calm the toothache. If the teeth have been hurt by an
acid, seltzer-water will reduce the irritation.

I have known a violent toothache cured
by applying, on the advice of a doctor, a
poultice composed of flour, white of egg,
brandy, and gum, at the angle of the lower
jaw, on the spot where one feels the beating
of the artery. It was a tooth in the lower
jaw, which was causing intolerable suffering.
Toothache may be caused by acidity of the
saliva, from which inflammation and irritation of the teeth arise. A strong solution
of bicarbonate of soda is the remedy for
toothache when produced by this cause.
Rinse the mouth well with this solution,
and apply a little bicarbonate of soda to
the teeth and gums with a brush. Try this
remedy when you suffer from toothache; and
if you find relief from it, you will have
discovered the cause of the pain. From
henceforth use bicarbonate of soda in brushing your teeth.

Several persons have assured me that they cured the decay of their teeth by the following means :—Fill the hollow teeth with alum powdered very fine ; as the alum melts in the tooth, the pain disappears. The operation must be repeated whenever the pain returns, and in the end it will be conquered and the decay stopped.

This decay is due to the destructive action of the particles of food which stick in hollow teeth, remain there, and become corrupt. Alum is known to be an antiseptic; hence its virtue in the cases which now occupy our attention.

Nevertheless, whenever it is possible have recourse to the dentist, and to a good dentist: for anything else is a foolish economy, which will cost a great deal more in the end, to say nothing of the needless worries, accidents, and sufferings.

Stopping, and especially gold stopping, done in time, may preserve our teeth indefinitely, and save us from horrible suffering.

All neglect on this point is reprehensible, and will often cause us infinite regret.

Tooth-Powders, Dentifrices, Elixirs.

If you are determined to use powders and elixirs, be very careful in your choice of them; I should even advise you to prepare them at home, to be quite sure that they contain neither cream of tartar, bole, or calcareous salts—all substances which would be fatal to the enamel of the teeth and to the purity of the breath.

Here are some recipes, of which I will guarantee the excellence, with which tooth-powders and elixirs can easily be prepared. I have the authority of doctors and chemists for them:—

(1) Carbonate of precipitated chalk ... 40 drachms.
    Powder of *Bol d'Arménie* ... 40 ,,
    ,, of magnesia ... ... 10 ,,
    Root of Spanish camomile ... 5 ,,
    ,, of cloves ... ... 5 ,,
    Bicarbonate of soda ... ... 4 ,,
    Essence of peppermint ... ... 1 drachm.
        Mix all together carefully.

(2) Powdered quinine ... ... 10 drachms.
    Tannin ... ... 10 „
    Charcoal ... ... 10 „

Pound them in a mortar, and keep in a china or wooden pot.

(3) Phosphate of dry chalk ... ... 2 ounces.
    Iris powder ... ... 1 ounce.
    Powdered myrrh ... ... 8 grains.

                 Mix these and add :—

    Solution of cocaine ... ... 1 drop.
    Eucalyptus oil ... ... 12 drops.

Mix and heat them all well together, and strain. This powder is very good for delicate teeth and spongy gums.

(4) Take precipitated chalk as a basis, and add :—

    Powdered soapwort ... ... 4 drachms.
    Eucalyptus oil ... ... 4 „
    Carbonic acid ... ... 4 „

An elixir recommended by a chemist :—

    Green anis ... ... $6\frac{1}{2}$ drachms.
    Cloves ... ... $2\frac{1}{2}$ „
    Cinnamon ... ... $2\frac{1}{2}$ „
    Quinine ... ... $2\frac{1}{2}$ „
    Root of Spanish camomile ... $2\frac{1}{2}$ „
    Essence of peppermint ... ... $1\frac{1}{2}$ „
    Cochineal ... ... 1 drachm.
    Alcohol (rectified 90°) ... ... 1 quart.

These various substances to be infused in the alcohol for a month, then filtered through paper.

Here is a mixture recommended by a good dentist, who prefers it to *eau de Botot* :—

Thymol	...	...	...	3 grains.
Benzoic acid	...	...	...	2 scruples.
Tincture of Eucalyptus		...	46 minims.
Water ...	...	...	...	12 ounces.

Shake the bottle.

The mouth should be rinsed with this mixture before going to bed. It is during the night that the mouth and teeth suffer most from the fermentation and secretions, which are formed more profusely during sleep. Thanks to this lotion, decayed teeth are purified, and can no longer become a source of destruction and suffering. The existing cause will have been eliminated and rendered powerless.

In the summer season the most delicious and the best dentifrice is the strawberry. It cleans the teeth to perfection. It should be bruised on the brush, the teeth rubbed with it, and then rinsed out with tepid water. An infusion made with the petals of the pink procures the best of elixirs also during the summer.   The pink is an antiseptic.

I recommend you to eat a small crust of bread at the end of every meal, after the dessert.

Tartar.

In spite of all washes and dentifrices, tartar will form, with rare exceptions, even on the most carefully kept teeth.   People subject to gout and rheumatism will find tartar forming on their teeth to some extent, in spite of all their care.

For those who have not this temperament, energetic brushing will at least in some degree prevent or delay, and sometimes even destroy, the appearance of tartar. Alum is ordered to prevent tartar.   Take a little on your brush, which should be very slightly wet, and brush your teeth with it every morning for three or four days at a time.   Rinse your mouth with honey and water afterwards, to correct the strong astringent.

But it is often necessary to resort to more vigorous measures for getting rid of the evil. Dr. Magitol, whose name is famous in the records of dentistry, does not hesitate to use the steel to deliver one from the dreaded tartar. Once the patient is in his hands, there is no way of escape ; and he does not let you go till he has made an end of the stony concretion which has formed on your teeth.

Your mouth is sometimes filled with blood, and you wish to stop the practitioner's hand, but he will not let you go till he has delivered you from this first cause of the destruction of the teeth.

The subsequent treatment is very simple. You have only to suck pastilles of chlorate of potassium ; but be sure that they are pastilles in which the preserving ingredient is not absent, as is often the case.

As to black teeth, it is perhaps dangerous to whiten them with the aid of chloric acid. Many conscientious dentists refuse to

F *

perform this operation. Salt may be tried
for this unpleasant growth which sometimes
invades the human teeth, if the person thus
inflicted is made too unhappy thereby.

With regard to salt, there is another
occasion on which it may be of great use in
connection with the teeth : if, after having
a tooth extracted, the mouth is filled with
salt and water, there need be no fear of
hæmorrhage.

Children's Teeth.

Care should be taken of the teeth from
the moment they begin to show themselves.
What a moment of suffering and pain for
the poor little ones—and for the mother,
who sometimes dreads fatal accidents at this
time !

The cutting of the first little teeth will
be facilitated by rubbing the poor baby's
gums with Narbonne honey. It will make
the flesh tender (at the same time strengthening the stomach and intestines), and the

teeth will come through without causing
the suffering which sometimes leads to convulsions, and even death. A crust of bread,
a root of marsh-mallow, the coral invented
by nurses, are all useful for promoting
dentition.

The importance of attending to children's teeth is evident to the meanest capa-
city. It has a double object—to prevent
suffering which they are at the moment too
weak to bear, and to ensure them good and
fine teeth in the future.

When the second teeth come, there are
often deleterious influences to be combated.
There is always more or less chance of
decay or of the formation of tartar; care
must be taken, advice asked, and precautions must not be neglected for putting a
spoke in the wheel of the evil in time. A
true mother will also watch over the growth
of the teeth as carefully. Dentists can correct by immediate attention all such dental
deformities as may begin to show themselves.

THE VOICE.

The Organ.

A PRETTY voice is a powerful attraction in a woman; and a fine masculine voice, full and sonorous, that has not yet undergone any change, is also very much to be admired.

We ought, therefore, to watch over the organ that Nature has bestowed upon us, so as to keep it in a good state and to improve it. A harsh voice may be softened by the force of will, of study, and of work. A loud crying voice can be subdued in tone, a rough one may be made gentler.

A woman should speak in a rather low voice, but distinctly. To shout in speaking denotes vulgar habits, and sometimes shows a domineering spirit; many people talk too loud for others to be heard in discussion, to prevent their opponents from expressing their thoughts fully, or to keep them from making some just or judicious remark. It is well not to spoil the tone of the voice by talking across a room or from the top of the house to the bottom, as is often done without any necessity. In doing so, both persons are obliged to shout at the top of their lungs to make themselves heard—a proceeding which must coarsen and wear out the voice at last.

There are people, too, who, when they are spoken to and do not quite take in what is said to them, pay no sort of attention, either from distraction or want of interest in what concerns others; the speaker has in that case to begin all over again, raising the voice to the highest pitch, which then becomes a habit, though often a useless one. These things generally happen in family life, where politeness and mutual consideration are so often wanting, and where they are more needed than anywhere else.

We should have self-command enough never to shout, even when under the influence of anger, indignation, or pain. Such outcries spoil for ever the chords of a musical voice.

Children should not be allowed to scream out when they are playing. I mean those strident screams, which are hideous, and which they so often give. When very little children scream in a fit of rage, it is well to throw a few drops of water in their faces, and go a little away from them without saying anything. They will then stop those screams which might be dangerous to such frail little creatures.

One doctor claims to have discovered a way of making all voices much more harmonious. He claims for peroxide of hydrogen the power of improving the voice in strength as well as in *timbre*. He inculcates, therefore, that it should be used by tenors, baritones, *prima-donnas*, etc., as well as by ordinary mortals desirous of possessing a voice of gold or of crystal. His theory is that the peroxide is a constituent of the air and the dew in Italy, and that the beauty and richness of trans-alpine voices are due to its presence. This doctor has invented a chemical compound to replace the air of Italy. After inhaling it, the voices of those who did so were said to be fuller, clearer, richer, and more mellow in tone.

Slight Diseases of the Throat.

How many voices are worn and hoarse from the effects of useless excesses and fatigues! What a drawback to a woman, and even to a man, is a hoarse, indistinct, disagreeable voice! And generally this evil might have been prevented, or at least remedied.

But there are some kinds of hoarseness which arise from involuntary causes; for instance, that which is caused by the larynx being too wide. It should then be contracted, to prevent the ugly hoarse tones so afflicting to a delicate ear. Lemon, orange-ade, and water acidulated with verjuice, are good in such cases; and cold drinks should always be used. A gargle of water and verjuice mixed may also be used with advantage.

If the hoarseness proceed from bronchitis or a slight quinsy, use a gargle made from the wild mustard (*sisymbrium officinale*). This herb is a tonic as well as an expectorant.

In every case of hoarseness it is better to talk as little as possible and in a very low tone, to drink barley-water, and to eat black-currant jelly. Nero is said to have drunk leek-water to keep his voice in good condition. Onions will have the same effect on our voices. Apples baked in their skins, pippins especially, are much recommended to orators; and everyone knows that many singers swallow, or are supposed to swallow, the yolk of a raw egg every morning before breakfast, to clear the voice.

Butter-milk refreshes the voice when it is fatigued.

Tobacco, alcohol, and all violent stimulants are bad for the voice. Hot, spiced, and savoury food should be avoided by those who care for the elasticity of their voice.

Recipes for Clearing the Voice.

The Arabs have a very agreeable remedy for aphonia. The patient till he is cured is fed on the pulp of the apricot, cooked in the ordinary way, and dried in the burning sun of Sahara.

If a slight irritation of the throat spoils the sweetness and musical sonority of your voice, gargle with salt-and-water (common salt). It is very good to inhale the steam of hot milk in which figs have been boiled, if you want to mellow the tone of the voice. Fumigations are also excellent. Mix a little powdered amber and myrrh together, put them on a red-hot shovel, and inhale the smoke.

An infusion of male veronica with a little sugar-candy is also recommended. A glassful should be taken before breakfast.

THE EYES.

The Language of the Eyes.

SOME eyes are so beautiful that they make one forget irregularity in the features, and even other physical defects. They exercise a fascinating and sovereign charm. Their power does not lie in their colour; it matters not whether they have borrowed the tint of the corn-flower or the flash of the black diamond, whether they reflect the June sky or hide their velvety softness under long lashes; it is the expression which makes them beautiful.

They must reflect a soul—a soul strong and great, tender, sweet, loyal and sure, ardent and loving. The inner being must

show itself in the eyes; we must feel, thanks
to them, that beneath this outer shell of
flesh there is an immaterial spirit, which an-
imates and will survive the material body.

If the eye is without expression, it is
because the individual soul is heavy and
asleep. Those lifeless eyes will never
awaken vivid and deep sympathies in
others; they will draw forth neither the
heart nor the intelligence; they will be
utterly powerless.

Some people like blue eyes, others adore
dark ones. There are certain conditions
necessary to the beauty of the eye; it should
be long, almond-shaped, and fringed with
long lashes. Some wish them to be gentle,
others demand that they shall flash. Above
all things, the eye should open wide, with a
fine, frank, direct look—a look which is not
afraid to meet the regard of others. I am
not in any way condemning, be it understood, the timid regard of a young girl who
turns away surprised and almost frightened

from a passionate glance; but I dislike a furtive, suspicious look.

It is well to give children the habit of looking you straight in the face: not insolently, but simply, and with the noble assurance and confidence that all honest beings should have in themselves and in others. Nor should enthusiasm and ardour be repressed in young creatures when it is excited by what is beautiful, and great, and good. If they are obliged to hide their delight, and still the beating of their young hearts, their looks will become subdued, and their eyes will lose their frank expression.

The most beautiful eyes are those which express all the feelings sincerely and directly. I know some that are good, tender, and sweet, but they can flash like lightning in moments of indignation or enthusiasm. These eyes can hide nothing; you may have confidence in those who have them.

Beware of the man whose eyes are impenetrable. He may not be actually a bad man, but he may become one. There are eyes which seem to flood one with light; others seem to have a veil drawn over them.

Those who know something of life divine the moral nature from the looks; and if we examine the eyes of others attentively, we shall not often be deceived in this world. We shall then know whether the being we are trying to decipher is artificial or loyal, frank or reserved, hard or tender, energetic or weak, keen or indifferent.

Two beings that love each other can speak with their eyes, and have no need of any other language. " Love," says an English poet, " springs from the eyes "; unfortunately he adds, rather frivolously, " like the potato," alluding to the germs or eyes of the tuber from which other potatoes grow. How often have we not heard it said, " One glance from her is enough to captivate and enslave me for ever " !

True, there are eyes so splendid in expression, so admirable in their limpid clearness, that they take hold of one's heart and soul, and it is impossible to resist them.

There are eyes so powerful that they almost hypnotise one. It is lucky if their fascination is only used for good.

In my opinion, eyes are only really beautiful if they reflect good and wholesome thoughts and noble sentiments. Righteous indignation does not diminish their attractiveness, and I like to see them burn with the fire of enthusiasm.

But let jealousy, cunning, envy, or brutal rage depict themselves in the eyes, and they will at once lose all their charm and power, no matter how perfect they may be in form and colour.

The Care of the Eyes.

But although it is true that the greatest beauty of the eyes lies in their expression, they must not be red, inflamed, tired, or without eyelashes, if they are to keep all their seductive fascination.

Never rub your eyes, if you do not want to have red eyelids. Even if something gets into your eye, do not irritate it by trying to get rid of the intruder by violent measures. Close your eyes quickly, and wait patiently thus even for a quarter of an hour, if necessary. The natural watering of the eye will expel the foreign substance.

If your eyes are red from the wind, bathe them in tepid water with a little common salt in it.

Veils, and especially spotted veils, are very bad for the sight. They should only be worn, therefore, in the winter months to protect the face from the cold.

Sitting up late, and artificial light, make the eyes red and tired. Lamps should always have large shades on them. It is dangerous to the sight to look at the sun or at the centre of an electric light. Gas, candles, and ordinary lamps should all be subdued by screens, smoked glasses, etc.

Do not amuse yourself by watching the play of the flames in the grate, or considering the designs formed by the red-hot coals. A screen is a necessity, even if you are sitting at one side of the fire.

White walls on which the light is vividly reflected, the snow, or roads whitened by the rays of the sun in summer, are very fatiguing to the eyes, unless they are protected by coloured glasses; on the other hand, some oculists consider these glasses injurious. Wide-brimmed hats, shading the forehead well, are the best headdress for the summer, as they protect the eyes from the fierce light and from the sun's rays.

However strong your eyes may be, grant them a little rest after two hours of continuous work, whether with the pen or the needle, etc. If they are weak, do not occupy them much with any work which involves fixing them on minute objects. Do not

write, read, sew, or do anything which demands an effort of the sight when the light
is insufficient. Whatever work you are
doing, close the eyes every now and then for
an instant. Let them wander to a distance,
too, at intervals.

The most restful colours for the eyes are
green and blue. Do not surround yourself
with very bright colours. Red is blinding.
Choose soft shades, very much blended, in
hangings, stuffs, wall-papers, etc.

Very dark shades are unsuitable either
for decoration or furniture, and strong con-
trasts are equally tiring to the eyes.

The light should come from the side, not
in front. In working, it should come from
the left-hand side.

You should write on tinted paper, and
only read books and newspapers that are
well-printed. Avoid stooping too much in
reading, writing, or sewing, etc., to avoid
congesting the head and face. It is bad
for the sight to read in the train, or while

driving and walking, or in bed when one is tired or recovering from illness.

Take care of the stomach. It is said that Milton became blind not only from overworking his eyes, but also because he suffered from dyspepsia. Living in a damp place often weakens the sight. Hygienic conditions are important for the eyes; sobriety and absence from all excesses have always been rewarded by excellent sight. But absence of good food would be as bad, on the other hand. Beware of too sudden changes from heat to cold, or from darkness to light. In consideration of this, beds should be placed in such a position that the eyes will not face the daylight or the sun's rays on first awakening. The light should come to them from the side. It is well to wait for a few moments in coming out of the dark into a brilliantly-lighted room before beginning to read, write, or work.

Montaigne. advises the application of a plain piece of glass on the page when reading, and in this way to delay the use of spectacles. Under the glass the paper of the book or newspaper is, in fact, less staringly white, and the characters appear more distinct. The light of the lamp should, of course, not be allowed to strike directly on the glass. Never rub your eyes on awakening, and prevent little children from acquiring this habit.

Use magnifying - glasses, microscopes, and eye-glasses as sparingly as possible, and take off your glasses whenever you can do without them—when out walking, talking, etc.

Bathe your eyes pretty often, especially morning and evening. If you are at all afraid of congestion, use tepid water. An infusion of weak black tea is good for bathing sore eyes.

Avoid all eye-washes that have not been prescribed by a good doctor or oculist. If your eyelids are inflamed, wash them with rose- and plantain-water. Strawberry juice

well strained through a cloth is also very
beneficial.

An experienced doctor recommends elder-
flower water for the pricking one sometimes
feels in the eyes. The juice of chervil and
of lettuce is also refreshing when the eyes
are irritable.

The following recipe is recommended by
a doctor :—A quart of soft water, a pinch
of kitchen salt, and a teaspoonful of good
brandy. Let them dissolve, and shake the
bottle before using the mixture. This wash
strengthens the sight quickly, and restores it
to its former vigour. The evening, says the
same doctor, is the best time for bathing the
eyes.

The Eye-lashes.

To be beautiful, and protect the eyes
well, eye-lashes should be long and thick ;
and under these conditions they give great
softness to the expression of the eyes.

It is asserted that a medicinal pomade,
called " pomade trichogene," will make them

grow. Some women have the points of
their eye-lashes cut by a practitioner, to
make them thick and long.

Rubbing the eyes is a bad habit in more
ways than one; it makes the lashes fall out.

I cannot advise blackening the lashes,
in spite of the attraction it may lend to the
eye. All making-up so near to the precious
organ of sight is doubly dangerous.

The Eyebrows.

Bushy eyebrows give something brutal
and fierce to the face. Very tiny fine combs
have been invented to keep them in good
order.

Fine arched eyebrows that look as if
they had been painted with a brush give
an air of serenity to the countenance. On
the other hand, rather thick eyebrows are
becoming to the eyes.

Scanty badly-formed eyebrows, which
make a red line over the eye, are a real defect.
Rubbing them every morning with a little

petroleum after bathing them in cold water
may help to make them grow. Cutting
them also makes them grow thicker.

If you wish to lengthen or darken your
eyebrows, I would advise, in spite of my
horror of making-up, a means which is absolutely harmless : a solution of Chinese
ink in rose-water. This is a secret of the
harem.

Further Advice.

It is asserted that squinting is often due
to the placing of the cradle where it receives
a bad or false light. The baby on awaking
is forced to squint.

A child's bed should therefore be placed
with discernment. The light should come
from the side, never in front or behind the
head.

Happily, strabism may be corrected or
entirely destroyed   We counsel those who
are so afflicted to submit to the treatment
which will restore their eyes to that straight-
ness of look which is their chief beauty.

The expenditure of time and money, even suffering, should deter no one. The result obtained will amply repay all the sacrifices made.

THE NOSE.

Abnormal Redness.

YOUR nose may be chiselled in the most exquisite manner, but if the roses of your cheeks have spread over it, you will wish that instead of your inflamed Greek nose you had a common snub one, if only it were quite white. And you would be right if there were no remedy for this little misfortune.

When a red nose is not due to the cold, but to the dryness of the nasal duct, or to the delicacy of the capillary vessels, it is easy to stop the inflammation. You prepare a wash in the following manner :—Powdered borax 154 grains, a teaspoonful of *eau de Cologne*, soft water 5 ounces. Melt the borax in the water, then add the *eau de Cologne*. It will be sufficient to damp the nose with this lotion, and to let it dry without wiping it. If the nose should begin to burn again, repeat the treatment. Here is another mixture, which does not differ very much from the first, but I give it, all the same. Dissolve 30 grains of borax in half an ounce of rose-water and the same quantity of orange-flower water. Wet the nose at least three times a day with this refreshing lotion, and do not wipe it off.

Redness of the nose often proceeds from a kind of congestion. In this case it should be washed with warm water only, on going to bed at night.

This unpleasant redness may also be imputed to the kind of constitution. Scrofulous persons are afflicted with it. They must abstain from ham, or pork under any form, meat, bacon, fat, and sausage-meat, and also from salt meats or highly-spiced foods.

Redness also comes from a bad state of the nostrils; in that case, wash with hot water. Cold water will increase the redness. Never touch your nostrils with your fingers. Sniff up a little hot water, and eject it gently. A little thick cream spread on the irritated part will protect it very much against the effects of the open air, and will soften the inflamed surface. A chill in the head will aggravate the evil, so the head should be covered during sleep.

Wearing the clothes too tight, especially the stays, and a feeble action of the heart, may also be the cause of a red nose. In the first case, it is evident the clothes should be worn loosely. In the second, a great deal of rest is necessary; while a cold bath on getting up in the morning, rubbing vigorously with a flesh-brush after it, will be found beneficial. Dry yourself well till the

G

skin is warm. Pure air is also a necessity at all times.

Hairs in the Nose.

The masculine nose of all kinds is often ornamented by hairs growing on the end of it. There is no reason why this inconvenient growth should not be pulled out with a pair of tweezers.

But this would be a dangerous method of getting rid of the hair which sometimes grows inside the nostrils; the inflammation caused by pulling out these hairs, or by using a depilatory, might endanger the shape, or even the existence, of this important olfactory organ. You must be content with cutting these unfortunate hairs, if you have them.

Small Black Spots.

As to the little black spots with which many noses (and sometimes cheeks) are spotted, I will not decide what causes them; whatever it is, the way to extirpate the secretion is to squeeze the black spot out between your fingers.

Washing with fresh water, or water with a few drops of tincture of benzoin in it, is advisable; also frictioning with diluted glycerine. A chemist recommends friction with soft soap. A doctor also prescribed this soap, put on in thin layers on the affected parts; this should be done going to bed at night.

The Science of Rhinoplasty.

This science, which concerns the nose, has made such progress that it is possible now to modify, even to change, the shape of the nose. The methods employed belong to the regions of medicine.

I may, however, suggest to persons afflicted with a large nose the means of diminishing its size. To do this, it will be sufficient to wear a *pince-nez*, without glasses in it, at night, and in the day-time whenever you are alone.

If the nose is a little on one side, or deviates from the central line, it must be blown *exclusively* on the defective side until it has become straight.

In New York the society women re-mould their noses, so as to make them Greek, Roman, or Jewish, according to their fancy, by means of an instrument worn at night.

THE EAR.

Its Properties.

I SHALL perhaps be thought to be going into very minute particulars if I insist on the necessity of cleaning the exterior of the ear, as well as the auditory duct, very carefully. Many scrupulously neat people, from not being able to see this part of their body in detail, and from using only a sponge and towel for washing it, do not succeed in perfectly clearing all the little corners of the

ear from dust or other matters that soil it.
A little ivory implement is necessary for the
purpose. It should be covered with the
corner of a wet towel, and it will penetrate
perfectly into all the turns and corners of
the pavilion and auricle, which should be
first soaped, and which fingers, however
delicate they may be, could not perfectly
accomplish. These ear - pickers, always
covered with a towel, serve to free the external auditory duct of the wax which is
necessary to the ear, but which accumulates
in useless and even harmful quantities, and
is very unpleasant to the eye if the excessive secretion is not carefully taken away
every day.

I have seen the most charming little ears,
the shape of a bean and lined with rose-
colour, but seeming profaned by want of
minute care in cleaning them. Instead of
being delightful to look at, as they might
have been, they presented an almost repulsive aspect. If this is so with a pretty ear,

what must it be in a commonplace or ugly one ?

Precautions for avoiding Deafness.

If you have any tendency to deafness, or even are a little hard of hearing, take great care not to wet your hair. You must not plunge into a cold bath—you should even wear an oiled silk cap in your bath.

If the inside of your ear is irritable, never scratch it with the head of a pin or hair-pin, the point of a pencil, or any analogous object.

If your ears are at all delicate, it is bad for the hearing to let your feet be cold. Beware of the damp for your extremities, and never sit with your back to an open window. Such imprudence will increase your infirmity.

Never pour any liquid into your ears which has not first been warmed. Neither should oil, milk, or other fatty substances, be used for relieving ear-ache. All the grease is liable to become rancid, and will only set up inflammation.

If a live insect gets into your ear, do not be alarmed ; the bitter wax will soon make it get out again. Besides, if you get a little warm water poured in the ear, the insect will be drowned, and will float to the surface, where it can be taken away with the fingers. A few puffs of tobacco-smoke, too, will stupefy this intruder into a place where he had no business to go.

Never box a child's ears; you might break the tympanum and cause incurable deafness by your brutality.

Acoustic Fan.

I wish to point out to women who have a certain form of nervous deafness a very simple and easy way of diminishing this dis- agreeable infirmity, which puts those who have it almost out of human fellowship by preventing them from hearing what is being said or taking part in conversation.

They should always have close at hand
a Japanese fan made of bamboo canes split
in two and covered with paper. When
they want to hear, they must at once take up
the fan, spread it out, leaving the wide edge
against the jaw (on the deaf side or on the
side next whoever is speaking), and spreading
it enough to stretch the bamboo canes to
some extent. These persons will be quite surprised to find that they hear as well as if
they were using an audiphone or a denta-
phone, to say nothing of the more pleasing
appearance of the fan.

THE HAND.

Its Beauty.

IT is supposed that one must have descended from a stock that has enjoyed five
centuries of leisure to possess a perfectly
elegant and aristocratic hand. I know not

whether the recipe is infallible ; it is certainly not within the reach of all.   We may,
however, console ourselves.   It is something
to have a white and delicate hand, to begin
with, even if it be not perfectly modelled ;
and this is quite possible even if we work,
occupy ourselves with our households, and
even do gardening : on condition, let it be
understood, that we take some pains and
trouble.

Do not fear, therefore, to put your hands
to whatever is wanted, and to use, for your
own service or that of others, the hands God
has given you.   You will be shown here how
to keep them soft and delicate, in spite of
any work you may be obliged to do.

The great ladies of other days set so
much store on the beauty of their hands
that one of them, the Countess de Soissons,
would never close them, for fear of hardening the joints.   What a martyrdom !   How
should we like to be condemned never to
use our ten fingers ?

G *

It was for the same reason that pages —and, later, lacqueys—were charged with carrying the prayer-books and other small objects which were found too heavy for the lily-white little hands of fine ladies.

In the eighteenth century the noble ladies made their servants open all the doors for them, for fear of widening their hands by turning the handles and pushing back the bolts.

The Marquise de Crégny was spoken of as a woman of astonishing resolution, "because," they said, "if she had not a lacquey near, she opened the doors for herself, without fear of blistering her hands"!

Little hands are more valiant nowadays. There are some that do not shrink from manipulating potter's earth with them ; and we congratulate those women of society who have a horror of the idleness in which their ancestors delighted.

If the hand is disfigured by warts or moles, these ugly growths must be destroyed

in the same way that I have pointed out
in the section on "The Face."

Care of the Hands.

Gloves should be worn while house-
keeping or gardening : old gloves that have
got loose from wear. They protect the
hands from the effects of the air, as well as
keep them clean, which obviates too frequent washing. Too much washing has its
drawbacks.

But there are certain employments which
forbid the use of gloves, and in this case the
hands must be washed when necessary. No
doubt; but then those corrosive soaps which
deteriorate the skin need not be used. *Savon
de Marseille*, white and pure, and slightly
scented, is the only soap to be recommended.
At the same time dilute a little oatmeal or
bran in tepid water for washing your hands.
If they are very much stained, use a little
borax or ammonia.

The roughest hands may be made soft

and smooth by a few minutes' care every night before going to bed. Five, or at the most ten, minutes will be long enough to efface the signs that even hard work may have left on our hands. A small, but very inexpensive, arsenal is necessary : namely, a nail-brush, a pumice-stone, a box of powdered borax, a bottle of ammonia, a pot containing fine white sand, and a lemon.

If you find that a kind of hard skin is forming on the inside of the hand, rub the place thus thickening as long and patiently as may be necessary with pumice-stone. This is important for preserving the softness of the hand and the delicacy of touch.

Stains can be removed either with the sand, borax, or ammonia, according to the nature of them.

All the lines on the palm of the hand which may have become filled with black and greasy substances, from contact with brushes and dusters, etc., must be perfectly cleaned. Have I said that to begin with

the hands must be well washed? I shall
point out further on how the nails should
be cared for.

When the hands are absolutely clean,
rub them with dry oatmeal, and wear gloves
during the night.

If glycerine has no bad effects on the
skin, it is preferable to oatmeal, and should
be used pure. The following mixture will
make glycerine suit everybody :—The yolk
of an egg, $1\frac{1}{2}$ drachms of glycerine, and $1\frac{3}{4}$
drachms of borax, well mixed. Anoint your
hands with this (which makes a kind of
pomade), and always cover them with
gloves.

The oatmeal may suffice, and is more
economical. White of egg in which alum has
been dissolved is also recommended : three-
quarters of a grain to one white of egg.

If the hands are in a very rough and
bad state, it would be well to use cold
cream at the beginning of the daily treatment we have advised. After using it

for a month, the hands will be in a good enough state to allow of the use of dry oatmeal only.

Hands that are not constantly employed in household work can be kept white by simply washing them night and morning in a clear *bouillie* of oatmeal.

A mixture of glycerine and lemon-juice in equal parts is also much thought of for preventing redness of the hands.

Here is a recipe for almond paste :— Take 1½ ounces of bitter almonds, and throw them into boiling water to divest them of their skins. Then dry them. Pound them in a mortar, or bruise them under a heavy bottle. Pound separately 1 ounce of iris root (if you have not an irritable skin) and 1 ounce of starch. Mix these with the pounded almonds; add 4 yolks of eggs, and mix them well in with the rest. Wet this paste with half a pint of spirits of wine and twenty drops of otto of roses. Heat this over a very gentle fire, stirring it continually with a spoon. This preparation should be kept in pots in a dry place. It becomes a powder, with which the hands are to be rubbed morning and evening.

This paste may also be made with flour of bitter almonds 8 ounces, oil of sweet almonds 1 pint, honey 16 ounces, and 6 yolks of eggs. The honey must first be melted separately, and then mixed with the almond-flour and eggs ; the oil is put in last, and all again well mixed together.

Cleansing of the Hands during the Day.

Never have soiled hands, but wash them without soap whenever it is possible. Lemon-juice will serve well for removing some stains. And if you wet a little salt with lemon-juice, there is no stain that this simple mixture will not obliterate.

A piece of fresh orange- or lemon-peel, if you have it at the moment, will take off tar well by rubbing with the outside of the peel.   The hands should be wiped at once to dry them.

Ripe tomatoes or strawberries, a sorrel-leaf, or a little milk, are all nearly as good as lemon-juice for removing ink-stains from the hands.

If you should happen to peel potatoes, your hands should be very dry for this work, and you must not wash them immediately after it.   By taking this slight precaution, the hands will not be stained by the juice of the tuber.

After peeling fruit and certain vegetables a little lemon-juice will restore the hands to a proper state ; they should first be made wet with water.

After any very rough work which demands vigorous washing, instead of using a solution of potash (above all, in winter), be sure to use petroleum jelly (real vaseline). This substance causes stains of all kinds to vanish.   Rub the hands with a little of the jelly : it penetrates into the pores of the skin,

and incorporates itself with greasy substances of any kind. Then wash the hands
with soap and hot water; this will make
them very soft, as well as very clean.

In this manner even hands " sanctified
by work" may still preserve an agreeable
appearance, which, I assure you, is not a
thing to be despised, especially when it is an
advantage so easy to obtain.

Damp Hands.

Damp hands are unsuitable for certain
kinds of work, and are, besides, repulsive to
touch. We must therefore be careful not to
rouse a feeling of repulsion against ourselves.

To give this kind of hand the requisite
dryness, the inside should be rubbed, several
times a day, with a cloth dipped in the
following preparation :—

Eau de Cologne ... ... 14 parts.
Tincture of Belladonna ... 3 „

If the hands are inclined to perspire too
much when you are exposed to great heat,

which happens in crowded receptions, plunge them into water in which a little powdered alum has been dissolved before putting on your gloves to go out into society.

Sun-burnt Hands.

People are often distressed at the end of the summer by the brown tint their hands have kept from the too fervent kisses of the sun.   Drawn on by the ever-increasing taste for outdoor pleasures, many young girls, and young women too, have given themselves up to croquet or lawn-tennis, to sailing and rowing in boats, with such ardour that they have forgotten to guard their little hands from the caresses of the great planet.   This does not much matter in the country or at the sea-side.   Brown hands, a little hardened inside, are almost suitable to the kind of life which demands the serge tailor-made dress and small hat or cap.   But how tanned and neglected they look surrounded by silk and lace !   It is then that regrets begin to be felt for not having worn large easy gloves while giving oneself up to the various sports.

We rush to remedies, but time will be the best of all for this. However, if you cannot resign yourself to wait, use lemon-juice and glycerine mixed, or a paste made of maize-flower and glycerine. A young lady-farmer of my acquaintance never uses anything but sour buttermilk. The acidity of this removes the stains and sun-burn of all kinds, and the oil contained in it is singularly good and softening to the skin. Nothing is so good as this buttermilk, especially if the hands are washed in it before going to bed, and gloves then worn during the night. Some persons only wash their hands in warm water to keep them clean during the day, and at night wet them with glycerine and rose-water, and sleep in gloves.

All the remedies that have been given for sun-burn of the face and freckles (*see* pp. 80 and 83) are equally applicable to the hands.

Fat Hands.

If your hands are rather fat, do not wear
tight sleeves. The pressure and discomfort
to the arm will only make the hand swell.
A tight cuff is as unsuitable to a large hand
as a low heel is to a large foot. If your
fingers are square or wide at the ends, you
may narrow them a little by pinching and
squeezing the tips. Needless to say, you
will not obtain the taper fingers you desire
all at once, but in time you will become
aware of a notable and pleasant change.

Chaps.

Chapped hands are a slight but very uncomfortable little evil which happens in
winter to children—and to grown-up people,
too, if they do not take much care of themselves.

And yet it is very easy to avoid this
suffering, which is due to the cracking of the
skin. To do so, we have only to be very

careful to dry the hands perfectly after washing them, and never to expose them while damp either to the cold or to the heat of the fire.

Women who look after the plants in their rooms, who comb their hair, or devote themselves to little employments of this kind, or to their households, wash their hands frequently; and as their time is precious to them, they do everything quickly and in a hurry. I advise them, with reference to the subject under consideration, to sacrifice a few moments in drying their hands thoroughly; they will more than save those moments in the long run, for the stiffness and pain caused by cracks will at last make all movements of their hands slow and awkward. When the hands have been dried with all possible care, they may be rubbed before the fire till they are quite soft and flexible.

Children should be made to take the trouble to dry their hands properly, as has

been advised.   It is pitiable to see the little
red chapped paws of most girls and boys. The
poor things suffer horribly from the cold
and from artificial heat; while if their hands
were properly taken care of, they would not
feel the changes of temperature at all to the
same extent.

The habit of rubbing the hands with dry
oatmeal before going to bed preserves them
from any disastrous effects of heat and cold
to which they may be exposed.   Cold water
should not be used for washing the hands;
it makes them more liable to chap; neither is
very hot water good for them.   People with
very thin skins should be extremely careful
to dry their hands well after washing them.
They should also cover them with a little
cold cream or vaseline, and wipe them again
after applying it.

If these counsels have been set at naught,
or not attended to in the manner which, I
can assure you, they deserve, the mischief
being done, here is the treatment you must

submit to in order to cure it. Take some vaseline or lard, sweet oil or tallow, and anoint your hands well after washing them in warm water. Whichever of these substances you choose, use it abundantly. Rub your hands well, twisting them about, rubbing between the fingers in and out for a good while, until they have become quite soft, and do not feel sore if you knock them against anything hard. Then divest them of the grease you have rubbed on them, and wash them with good soap and in warm water, with a few drops of ammonia in it. It is necessary to change the water several times. After this, rub your hands with the following mixture:—Glycerine, soft water, and eau de Cologne, in equal parts. When this operation is over, the hands will be very soft, and not the least greasy or sticky, as might be supposed.

I have seen hands that looked exactly as if they had been boiled, their owner having been obliged to do laundry work for several days continuously. She suffered much, the stretched and corroded skin of her hands being very painful; by using the foregoing prescription her hands became smooth and white again.

An English physician recommends the following for preserving delicate hands from chapping :—

Boric acid ...   . 30 grains.
Glycerine ...   . 2½ drachms.
The yolk of one egg well beaten.

Spread this on the hands, several times a day, before they are chapped. If you have the slightest scratch, do not use this remedy.

Here are some more ointments and liniments for these unpleasant cracks. They can be used for any part of the body where this cracking of the skin shows itself.

(1) Bees' wax   ...   . 3 parts.
    Olive oil   ...   . 4 ,,

Cut the wax into little pieces, put them into the oil, and melt them in an enamelled saucepan over a very slow fire. Anoint the chapped parts every night with this mixture. If it is the hands that are affected, wear gloves; if it is any other part of the body, cover it with a towel.

(2) Butter of cacao ... ... 4 scruples.
    Sweet-almond oil ... ... 4 „
    Oxide of zinc ... ... 2 drachms.
    Borate of soda ... ... 1½ grains.
    Essence of bergamot ... ... 8 drops.
(This liniment is very good for the lips too.)

(3) Take a handful of very pure linseed-meal and a teaspoonful of oil of bitter almonds; mix these two ingredients well together, then add warm water enough to make a light *bouillie* of them. Plunge your hands into this liquid, and rub them in it for about a quarter of an hour, then rinse them in tepid water.

Bitter-almond oil is prepared by mixing half a drachm of essence of bitter almonds with one pint of olive oil.

By using these simple remedies you will

cure the evil you would not take the trouble
to prevent. The last recipe may be used not
only for chapped hands, but for getting rid
of chilblains that are not broken ; this is
another of the ills of winter of which we are
now going to speak.

Chilblains.

Chilblains are even more to be dreaded
than a chapped skin.

A weak constitution or bad food predispose one to this affection. People subject
to it should walk a great deal, exercise their
hands, rub with alcoholic preparations the
parts where the chilblains are not broken,
and keep their hands and feet very
warm.

It might be thought that the hands
ought to have no more need of covering than
the face. Nevertheless, when it is very cold
everyone feels the necessity of sheltering
them from the biting frost and wind.
People with a slow circulation should wear

gloves the moment the temperature begins
to fall.

Yet it is often in mild and damp winters
that certain constitutions suffer most from
chilblains. There are many remedies for
this unbearable, though not dangerous, infliction, which spoils the prettiest hand in
the world :—

(1) Crush lily bulbs, and put them into
a vessel containing walnut oil. Apply this
under fine cloths to the parts affected.
(This is an excellent recipe.)

(2) Brittany honey will heal open
chilblains. Put it on the sore places, and
cover them up with fine white linen.

(3) Wrap the hands up in poultices
during the night, and in the morning rub
them with tincture of benzoin 2 ounces,
honey 1 ounce, and water 7 ounces, well
mixed.

(4) Wash ulcerated chilblains with tincture of myrrh very much diluted with tepid
water.

(5) Anoint broken chilblains with *pommade à la Sultane* (*see* p. 138), and cover with a fine white cloth.

It is difficult to cure chilblains during the winter if they have once broken ; it is well, therefore, to avoid coming to this pass by using the following remedies, which are all suitable for unbroken chilblains :—

(1) Steep the affected parts several times in a little spirits of salt weakened by a great deal of water.

(2) One doctor recommends a solution of permanganate of potash for destroying chilblains.

(3) Another prescribes this treatment: —Before getting into bed, put your hands into mustard and water, then apply a liniment composed of camphor and oil of turpentine.

(4) Constipation should be avoided, and all the functions of the body should be kept in good order. Women who are predisposed to chilblains should avoid wearing very tight sleeves, which impede the circulation, make

the hands cold, and in consequence bring on
the slight but disagreeable disorder of which
we are speaking. Chilblains may be prevented from making their appearance if the
hands are rubbed with a slice of lemon after
every washing. (This is good for preventing chapped hands also.)

(5) Infuse thirty long cayenne peppers in
twice their weight of rectified spirits. Keep
the infusion in a warm place for a week;
you will thus obtain a strong tincture.
Then dissolve gum-arabic in water till it is
the thickness of syrup; you must have the
same quantity of this as of the tincture.
Stir the two preparations well together, until
the mixture becomes cloudy and opaque.
Having procured some leaves of tissue-paper,
cover the surface of one with the mixture,
and let it dry; then apply a second layer
over the first. If the surface is brilliant after
the second drying, the two layers will
suffice; if not, add another layer. The paper
thus prepared is intended (when slightly

damped on the shiny side) to cover up the
red, swollen, and burning fingers.

(6) Wash the hands in mustard and
water. Dissolve Dijon mustard or any
other kind in warm water.

(7) One-half part of sulphuric acid, two
of glycerine, three of water. (Have this
prepared by a chemist. The bottle must be
labelled poison.) Wash the parts attacked
with this water.

(8) One ounce of salts of ammonia, one
ounce and a half of glycerine, eight ounces
of rose-water; shake well till the substances
are dissolved and mixed. Use as a wash.

(9) Wash your hands two or three
times a week in salt and water.

(10) Cut two turnips in slices, and pass
them through a strainer with three large
spoonfuls of very pure axunge. Apply this
at night, and cover with a white cloth.

(11) Infuse a handful of tan in tepid
water, and dip your hands into it for some
instants.

(12) Make a decoction of a pinch of laurel-leaves in a quart of water. Wash the hands every morning with this a little warmed.

(13) At the first sign of redness or irritation, wash with this mixture :—Five parts of essence of rosemary and one part spirits of wine.

(14) Wash with spirits of wine at 90°, in which crystallised phenic (carbolic) acid has been dissolved, in the proportion of 1 part to 9 parts of spirit. Use a stopper of linen. It should be applied as a compress, and kept on all night.

Vinegar with a fourth part of camphorated spirits added to it will prevent chilblains from appearing.

All that we have said on the subject about chilblains applies equally to the hands and feet.

The Care of the Nails.

Beautiful nails are looked upon as a precious gift. They should have a white

crescent at the root, and they should be as
rosy as the dawn. Pretty nails have been
compared to the onyx by poets—and, indeed,
in Greek, *onyx* means nail. Here is the
legend which, according to mythology, gave
its name to this particular kind of agate :—
One day Cupid, finding Venus asleep, cut
her nails with the iron of one of his arrows,
and flew away ; the parings fell on the sand
of the shore, and as nothing belonging to a
celestial body can perish, the Fates collected
them carefully, and changed them into
this quasi-precious stone which is called
onyx.

The women who have recourse to mani-
cures will tell you that the ugliest nails can
be improved by taking the trouble to push
the hard skin that grows at the base : an
operation which should never be done except
after soaping the hands in warm water, and
by means of an ivory or bone implement.
The edges of the nail should also be filed
in a gentle curve, following the outline of

the finger-end. The surface of the nail, too, should be polished.

One hour in the week given up to the care of the nails would suffice to keep them in good order, if they are brushed and cleaned conscientiously every day. They should never, for instance, be cleaned with a sharp-pointed instrument, like a pin; it hardens the nail, and only renders it more liable to retain the dirt that collects under it. Nothing is better than a lemon for cleaning the nails; stick the ends of the fingers down into it, and turn them in it again and again. Lemon also prevents the skin from growing up over the nails. It is very good for "upstarts," or the little loose jags of skin which only form at the base of badly-kept nails.

The use of cold cream or vaseline at night is very good for the nails; it softens them, and therefore keeps them from breaking and from looking dull.

I have been given a recipe which is said

H

to be very efficacious in hardening the nails. (Hardness is one of the conditions of a nail's beauty.) You melt over a very slow fire 5 drachms of walnut oil, $2\frac{1}{2}$ scruples of white wax, 5 scruples of colophony, and 1 scruple of alum. This ointment, which should be well beaten over the fire, is used at night.

A few implements are necessary for taking care of the nails : an ordinary nail-brush, a smaller one for getting in under the nails, a file, a polisher, and curved scissors—a special pair for each hand, as it is not possible to cut the nails of the right hand with scissors meant to cut those of the left.

Gloves.

The hand should feel comfortable in the glove, so as not to appear shortened or stuffed into it. The fingers of the glove ought to be as long as the fingers of the hand.

Gloves too tight do not wear well, which is an economical consideration ; and true elegance and intelligent *coquetterie* should always be blended with good sense.

Kid gloves wear better and longer if you know how to put them on for the first time. "It is quite a science," says a charming woman of my acquaintance. Your hands should be perfectly clean, dry, and fresh. Never put on gloves when your hands are damp or too warm. I have already pointed out a remedy for moist hands. (*See* p. 193.)

In putting on a pair of new gloves, the four fingers should be first inserted in the glove, leaving the thumb out, and the body of the glove should be turned back over the hand. When the fingers are quite in by means of the gentle movements of the other hand, introduce the thumb with the greatest care, leaning your elbow on your knee for support. Then turn back the glove on the wrist, and button the second button first, going on thus to the top. When this is done, come back to the first button, and you

will find that it will button easily, without
cracking the kid : which so often happens if
one begins with the first button. Besides,
it prevents the button-hole from widening :
an important matter if you wish the glove
to look well to the last.

Never pull off your gloves from the ends
of the fingers, but from the wrist. They
will then be turned inside out, which is
very good for allowing any moisture they
may have absorbed from the hand to
evaporate. When they are dry they can be
put back into their place, as says the old
song of St. Eloi. If you do not take the
precaution of airing gloves in this way, they
will shrink, and be difficult to put on again.
The kid will split with the slightest strain,
and the gloves be of no use.

Gloves should not be rolled up inside
each other. They should be stretched out
their full length in a box or perfumed
sachet. The light gloves should lie between
two pieces of white flannel, to preserve them

from contact with the dark ones, so that the
dye of the latter may not come off on them.

Black kid gloves can be renovated by
mixing a few drops of good black ink in a
teaspoonful of olive-oil. Apply it with a
feather, and dry them in the sun. Light
gloves can be cleaned with flour if they are
only slightly soiled. If they are much
soiled, use benzine, even with *suède* gloves.
When you buy gloves, examine the seams
well. If the thread shows white places
when stretched, do not buy the gloves; the
kid will easily tear; they will wear badly
and never look well.

Silk and woollen gloves are much
warmer than kid. In very cold weather
fur or woollen gloves should be worn over
suèdes.

The Arm.

The feminine arm should be round and
white. Those who have thin arms can
soon increase their size by energetic friction.

A hairy arm should be treated in the same manner as a lip with down on it. A red arm must be rubbed with almond-paste and honey.

Although I do not much like cosmetics, there is one I may mention for the neck and arms when wearing a low dress. You should get it made up by a chemist; it is very harmless, and free from danger :—Glycerine, rose-water, and oxide of zinc. This preparation has the advantage of not coming off on the black coats of your partners.

THE FOOT.

Conditions of Beauty.

WHEN a foot is well made, the boots and shoes wear well, and the walk is generally harmonious and graceful.

But the most charming foot may be disfigured by a boot that is too short or too narrow. And an ugly foot will become still worse if the owner tries to diminish its proportions by compressing them.

We must keep the foot Nature has bestowed upon us ; we shall only subject ourselves to useless tortures by trying to wear boots and shoes that were not made for it, and, far from remedying its defects, we shall only add others that it has not got.

The foot in ancient sculpture is perfectly beautiful, because it had never been subject to constraint in the sandal or slipper without heels. In our era it is only in the East, especially in Japan, that the human foot can be seen in all its beauty and grace. In the Empire of the Rising Sun the extremities have never known any bonds. The covering of the feet was there made for the comfort of the foot, and followed its outlines exactly. But now the European costume is being adopted in the country of the Mikado, and we are about to impose upon

them our abominable modern boots and
shoes, which deform the feet, because they
are not suited either to the structure of the
feet or to the movements they make in
walking.

The very pointed boots and shoes have
given birth to a great deal of suffering, and
to many infirmities which have spoiled the
foot and the walk.

Here are some counsels of healthy
coquetry; but will they be listened to?

You must not try to make your foot
smaller; you will only thicken it. Besides,
a very small foot is not well made. The
foot should be in just and harmonious
proportion to the body. A rather long foot
is the most elegant, as it appears narrow.
It is absurd to compress a wide foot; you
only make it more ugly, subject it to
excruciating pain, and lose the ease and
grace of your walk.

It is said that English and German
women have such large feet because they

drink a great deal of beer. The Americans,
who have also adopted that drink, are beginning to lose the beauty of their feet.
In wine countries—France, Spain, Italy,
etc.—where the women are indeed very
temperate, their feet are very delicate and
refined.

How to choose Boots and Shoes.

If the foot is narrow and a little too
long, the boot or shoe should be short in
the toe, and laced or buttoned down the
front. An ornament on the top of the
shoe diminishes the length of the foot in
appearance.

A short fat foot demands a long boot,
buttoned or laced at the side.

A very flat foot requires rather high
heels. If, on the contrary, your foot has
that high arched instep which is seen in
greatest perfection among the Arabs, and is
considered a mark of blue blood by the
Spaniards, it is not necessary to exaggerate

H *

the curve by high heels, which shortens
disadvantageously the foot that has no need
of shortening, and throws it out of its
necessary equilibrium.

The *Molière* shoe, which makes the
ankle appear thick, and cuts in two the
arch of which we have just been speaking,
should be abandoned in the name of æsthet-
icism. The low-cut shoe is, on the contrary, very graceful and becoming.

The Wellington boot is altogether un-
acceptable. The *brodequin* and kid boot
should reach higher than the ankle. No
other boot is fit for winter wear, as the
ankles must be protected from the cold. A
black boot is the only really pretty one; but
if made of stuff, it will add to the size of
the foot much more than in leather or kid.

A white shoe should only be worn on a
faultless foot. And, indeed, it is best to
wear shoes a shade darker than the dress.
A white shoe enlargens and widens the
foot.

An open shoe may be worn in various colours which are forbidden in a boot. All the same, it is well to choose a colour that matches the dress, but is a little darker. Black shoes and black stockings diminish both the length and breadth of the foot.

Women with thick ankles should wear stockings with embroidery high up on the sides in the length, not across the width : it will make the ankles appear smaller. When strong boots are worn with a light and elegant toilette, it is a sign of the very worst taste. If you cannot have nice boots and shoes, you should wear quiet and simple dresses.

Trying on Boots and Shoes.

I advise all those to whom it is possible to have their boots and shoes made for them. But if you do buy them ready-made, try them on in the evening. The feet are then spread out to their full size, and are at their highest degree of sensitiveness. The activity and exercise they have had during the day will have given them their fullest dimensions. The muscles will be tender from use, and the flow of blood in the arteries will be increased. The weight of the body affects the circulation in the feet to such a degree that people who are obliged to stand for a long time find that their feet enlarge very much. It is to the weight of the body when standing for a length of time that varicose veins are due, and people whose fibres are easily relaxed are specially subject to them. In good health the feet recover their normal size when one has been in bed for a few minutes, because they have then no longer to bear the weight of the body.

Try on your boots and shoes in the evening, therefore, when your feet are tired, and with comparatively thick stockings on. You will then find that you have plenty of room in your boots when your feet are fresh and you have put on very fine stockings.

Never take long walks with quite new boots on. Wear them in the house first for a few days, and then when you go out for a short time.

If you take these precautions, you will procure as much comfort for your feet in new boots as in old ones ; and boots, shoes, and slippers will all wear much longer.

A well-cut pair of shoes may be known by the following sign :—When the shoes are placed beside each other, they should only touch each other at the toes and heels. The soles should follow the line of the foot, so that it can rest its whole width on it comfortably.

How to take care of the Feet.

The feet should be washed every day, and by rubbing with pumice-stone, all thickening of the skin on the heel, sole, and toes should be made to disappear. I have said the feet should be washed every day : this must not be taken to mean the foot-bath.

The daily repetition of a foot-bath does not suit everybody. A foot-bath in which you keep your feet for ten or fifteen minutes is frequently injurious; above all, if it is taken very hot, or even warm. It has the bad effect of making the feet too tender, besides having a deplorable effect on the brain and sight if you are weak or delicate.

After washing your feet, and while they are still wet, rub the sole with dry salt, and then wipe them vigorously. This will strengthen them, and preserve them from the cold.

Warm your feet by walking. Foot-warmers of all kinds are bad both for beauty and health. They make you likely to have varicose veins in the legs. When you travel in very cold weather, wear over your shoes long stockings in the train or carriage, to prevent chilblains on your feet. Snow-boots are even better, but they are more difficult to carry about when you take them off on leaving the carriage. Light *sabots* are

indispensable in the country for going into
the garden in damp weather. Goloshes and
india-rubbers are equally good for keeping
the feet dry. All these—socks, snow-boots,
sabots, etc.—must, of course, be taken off the
moment you go into the house.

A bath of lime-tree flowers is very soothing to tired feet.

If the feet are tired from long standing,
a bath of salt and water is excellent for
them. Put a handful of common salt in four
quarts of water, as hot as can be borne without pain. Place your feet into this, and
with your hand splash the water over your
legs up to the knees. As soon as the water
cools, rub hard with a rough towel. (This
treatment, applied morning and evening,
will cure neuralgia in the feet.)

It is also advisable, when the feet are
swollen from a long walk or much standing,
to bathe them in water in which charcoal
has been boiled. The water should be
strained through a cloth before putting the

feet into it. Swelling and fatigue will both disappear rapidly. Alcoholic friction is also very good.

If the feet perspire, here is a good way of getting rid of this inconvenience :—Wash with boric acid in the water, and then powder the feet with dust of lycopodium. You may also try the following :—Salicylic acid three parts, talc seven, starch nine. These three substances should be well pounded and mixed, and the feet should be well powdered with the mixture. In some cases it will suffice to sprinkle the inside sole of the shoe with boric acid. In all cases I advise medical consultation before using any remedy. I believe my recipes to be inoffensive, but I know that it is sometimes dangerous to stop this perspiration. One thing may be done without fear of any kind —namely, to change the shoes and stockings two or three times a day.

In-growing Nails.

This is a very painful infirmity. If the nails of the great toes—and, indeed, all the nails—are cut quite square and not almond shape, you will not have to undergo suffering of this kind. However, once the evil is there, the question is how to cure it. Make a soft paste of mutton suet, Marseilles soap, and powdered white sugar, in equal parts. Apply this till the flesh recedes from the nail.

Or wet the whole foot, and after drying it well, apply a solution of gutta-percha and chloroform on the part affected. This operation should be repeated several times on the first day—say, about four times. The following day the number of applications may be diminished.

Here is the formula for the solution :—

| Chloroform | ... | ... | ... | 80 parts. |
| Gutta-percha | ... | ... | ... | 10 „ |

Another remedy is as follows :—Loosen the flesh round the nail, and cut the latter ; paint the suffering part with a small paint-brush dipped in perchloride of iron. The flesh is thus made hard and less sensitive. This is an infallible remedy.

Corns.

What an infliction ! Happily, they are not without a remedy, whatever the cause by which they are produced.

A shoe that is too wide is almost as destructive as one that is too narrow. If the foot is not properly supported by the shoe, it rubs continually against the leather in moving, and this friction predisposes to corns, almost as certainly as compression of the foot.

If a corn has only recently grown, you can get rid of it by rubbing it with pumice-stone.

At first, while the corn is still some-what tender, it can be got the better of by

applying wool dipped in castor-oil or leaves
of red geranium steeped in oil.

A poultice of the crumb of bread which
has been steeped in vinegar for thirty
minutes will cure a new corn in one night.

Good results are also to be obtained by
dissolving a false pearl in vinegar; the
creamy substance thus obtained is applied
to the corn (*pace* Cleopatra!). A soft rag
should be steeped in the cream, and carefully wrapped round the corn for the night.

Orpine, a patent remedy, is applied on
hard corns, which it softens, and thus facili-
tates their extraction. A raw onion bruised
has the same virtue, as well as ivy-leaves
steeped in vinegar. The leaf further serves
to protect the surface of the corn. A little
plaster-of-Paris damped (in paste) will
answer the same purpose; so will a little
circle (pierced in the centre) of agaric or
touchwood (from the oak or touchwood-tree)
put over the corn, which will thus be kept
from the pressure of the shoe. But here

are more scientific prescriptions for ointments which will destroy hard corns. They
are more or less like each other, but the
slight variations among them may just
make them suitable for divers kinds of
corns :—

(1) Salicylic acid	...	...	1 drachm.
Atronine	...	...	1½ grains.
Flexible collodion	...	...	1 ounce.

(2) Salicylic acid	...	...	5 drachms.
Extract of cannabis indica	...	½ drachm.
Collodion	...	...	4 ounces.

(3) Salicylic acid	...	...	15 grains.
Extract of cannabis indica	...	8 „
Alcohol at 90°	...	...	15 minims.
Ether at 62°	...	...	40 „
Elastic collodion	...	...	80 „

(Prescription of P. Vigier.)

Whichever of these three prescriptions
you choose, mix the divers ingredients, and
keep them in a well-corked bottle. The
remedy should be applied by means of a
camel's-hair brush dipped in the mixture,
and should be passed over the corn at least

twice. The applications should be made daily during not less than a fortnight. At the end of this time (during which you will be reduced to washing your feet with a damp sponge, which must not touch even the toes on which the corns are) the little tumours will be easily removed with your fingers after keeping the foot in warm water for an hour.

Bunions, which particularly affect the big and little toes, and sometimes the instep (in which case high heels should be at once renounced), can be cured in several ways :—

(1) If it is inflamed, cover it with a poultice and wear easy slippers. Then anoint the suffering part with an ointment composed of 7 parts of iodine mixed with 30 of lard.

(2) Cover the bunion with a piece of oiled silk over a layer of axunge.

(3) Take a piece of wash-leather, and make a hole in it large enough for the

bunion, put it on the bad place, and cover
it with oiled silk. Over this silk rub the
bunion twice a day with the ointment of
iodine and axunge.

(4) A piece of diachylon plaster has
a very good effect. You can also cut the
corn and cauterise it with sulphate of
copper, which is sold in sticks, like
nitrate of silver.

Cramp in the Foot.

The cramp is a most disagreeable infirmity.

If the toes are not perfectly free in the
boot or shoe, the constraint gives rise to the
most horrible cramp.

The cramp which so many people are
subject to at night is prevented by raising
the pillow. You place under the feet
at the head end of the bed a block about
the thickness of two bricks. Relief is immediate, certain, and lasting.

It is said—and I know it by painful

experience—that prescriptions of which arsenic forms even the smallest part cause terrible cramp in the calf of the leg.

Some useful Precautions.

When you come in with your leather boots wet, take them off at once, and have them filled with very dry hay. This absorbs the damp rapidly, stretches and fills out the boots, and so prevents them from stiffening and losing their shape. Above all, avoid putting them near the fire. The next day the hay is taken out, and may be dried for another occasion or thrown away. By stuffing the boots with paper you will obtain exactly the same result.

Paraffin softens boots that have stiffened from a wetting, and restores all their suppleness. Strong shooting-boots can be softened by exposure to broom-smoke, and by rubbing with olive-oil and lard. They will thus be much more comfortable, last twice as long, and will protect the feet better from the cold and damp.

If you want to make the soles of your boots more durable and impervious to water, warm them slightly, cover them with a coat of varnish, and dry it. Warm them again, varnish, and dry ; repeat a third time under the same conditions.

A mixture of cream and ink is excellent for keeping kid boots in good order.

A harness varnish may also be used for the same purpose. Take a very little on the end of a rag, and rub the boot well all over. Polish it with a bit of cloth. In countries where oranges are cheap, they are used for blacking the boots. The orange is cut in two, the juicy side rubbed on a black saucepan, and then on the boot. It is then brushed with a soft brush, and a brilliant polish obtained.

To prevent boots from creaking or cracking, the soles should be well saturated with linseed-oil. Place the boots on a dish full of oil; the sole will absorb the oil, which will also make it impervious to snow or water.

How to put on Laced or Buttoned Boots.

The feet of stockings should be longer than the feet they cover. They should be well pulled out at the toe, so that the heel can get into its place properly. (They will wear all the better for this precaution.) The bit that is beyond the toes in length should be turned back on them, to stretch the stocking, and all will arrange itself admirably as soon as you walk a little. (When evening comes, the foot of the stocking is no more too long.)

Very few persons know how to lace their boots and shoes; at least, they do not lace them the right way. Generally, people pull the lace as hard as they can, without noticing that they are making their foot very uncomfortable. You should place your heel well down in the shoe, then move your toes about in a satisfactory manner. After these preliminaries, put your heel on a chair opposite to the one you are sitting on, and then lace your boot. On the instep, lace the boot as tightly as possible, but tighten it gently and by degrees, so as to keep the foot well in the boot, in which your toes are quite at their ease. At the ankle, lace your boot so as to give every possible ease and comfort to that part of the foot.

Proceed in the same way with buttoned boots ; do not button the two buttons near the toes first. Button from the instep up to the ankle, to begin with, and before buttoning up the ankle itself, come back and do the first two buttons ; then finish by imprisoning, but as loosely as is possible, the lower part of the leg, the over-compression of which is so very bad for the health.

UNDERCLOTHING.

A TRUE woman, who always has the instinct of elegance and of allowable coquetry, will not be content with having fresh and dainty only her outside garments —those that can be seen, such as dresses, bonnets, mantles, etc.—but her under-clothes—those that cannot be seen—will be just as correct, in quite as good condition, and even more scrupulously neat.

I have been told that when bustles were the fashion some great ladies procured for themselves this abnormal development, so hated by artists, by means of worn-out old muffs, old aprons rolled up into bundles, and by all sorts of similar and strange devices.

On the other hand, little sempstresses economised in their outer garments in order to afford themselves crinoline bustles, which they cast off the moment they were soiled or out of shape.

Dressmakers declare that women in society are not ashamed to send them for patterns bodices the linings of which are horribly soiled and greasy, and which show that they have never undergone the little repairs always necessary after some little usage.

I have seen satin petticoats frayed and ragged, and others encrusted with mud, appear under superb gowns when these were held up. This is indeed ignoble.

Undergarments may be simple, but they should be as irreproachable as, or more so than, the dress, which even one spot disgraces. They should be as gracefully cut as possible ; and if they can be cut out of very good material, so much the better. But rather than have only a scanty or in-sufficient stock, it is better to have less ex-pensive material and the necessary quantity.

Happily, the taste for underclothing

made of coloured surah silk or cambric has
lost ground for some time back. Many
women of refined tastes, indeed, never gave
up white linen or cambric, or even simple
calico, which can be so easily washed,
whether the washing is done at home or
given out, and which comes back sweet and
fresh, to be put away in the wardrobes.

Chemises made of printed cambric, or
pink, blue, and mauve surah, have, to my
thinking, this drawback—they cannot be
thoroughly washed. Moreover, they are in
somewhat doubtful taste.

A virtuous woman has a repugnance to
excessive luxury in her underclothing. She
does not like too much lace or embroidery
or ribbons and bows. She has them
trimmed, of course, but with a certain
sobriety which speaks in her favour; she
likes them to be elegant, assuredly, so far
as she can afford it, but she denies herself
the abuse of and over-richness of trimming.

She prefers comparatively simple under-

linen, which there is no fear of washing,
and which can be changed daily. What
can be more refreshing than to put on
fresh linen?

Coloured stockings begin to be less worn
in summer, and only with shoes. With
boots, we are coming back to white thread
or cotton stockings—a habit much appreciated by women of refined habits, and who
understand true elegance.

The Corset and its Detractors.

The corset has a great number of
detractors in the male sex.

Some say it deforms a woman's figure;
others that it destroys her health.

"Look at the statues of antiquity," they
cry,—"those masterpieces which represent
the human body in its true beauty, as it
came from the hands of Nature. Have the
Venuses a narrow waist like the modern
woman? No, no; that divine form has
not been spoiled by any hindrance or

constraint ; it is freely developed and
expanded ; the goddess can bear children,
and transmits her perfect health to her
sons."

Charles X., who remembered the long
wasp-like bodice of Marie Antoinette, was
a fierce enemy to the corset.

A learned man of my acquaintance
declares that the corset has so flattened our
sides—which, according to proper osteology,
ought to be curved—that the feminine
skeleton is so much altered that in ages to
come it will considerably puzzle those who
excavate our tombs.

Tronchin, a Genoese physician, attributed the greater number of women's
diseases of his day to the corset; and to
diminish the evil he made people adopt
the Watteau pleat, under which the horrible
instrument of torture invented by stupid
coquetry can be loosened.

How many husbands still hold up to
their wives the example of Madame Tallien,

who all her life disdained to confine her
pretty figure in a prison of whalebones and
satin, and who was considered, in spite of
—or, rather, because of—this, the most attractive woman of her time !

The Good Points of the Corset.

Detractors of the corset are quite right
to blame the fools that do indeed deform
their bodies and destroy their health to
diminish their waists by an inch : an infini-
tesimal advantage, especially if we consider
the price paid for it—compression of the
vital organs, inconvenience in breathing,
congestion of the face, restriction of the
hips. (There are women who go so far as
thus to imperil their powers of maternity.)

But, on the other hand, if the corset is
only looked upon by woman as a support to
her frail figure, it becomes useful. She will
then have known how to give suppleness
and elasticity enough to assure comfort as
well as to allow of perfect liberty; that is

to say, perfect grace and movement. The
figure will undulate and balance itself like a
sapling bending to the wind, and will no
longer afflict us by recalling a knight in
steel armour.

The corset is absolutely necessary for a
very stout woman. It controls the exuber-
ance of her bodice, and it is impossible for a
fat woman to have any pretence to being
well-dressed without it. She will not appear
dressed at all, and, what is worse, she will
have a *débraillée* air.

The corset supports the petticoats, which
would otherwise lay too heavily on the
waist; and a very thin or even slight
woman will have no style without its help.
There will be something disjointed in her
whole look, in the slightest of her movements.

The corset has yet one more good side.
It serves as a support to the bust, the fibres
of which would become distended; and it
would soon fall too low if this kind of

I

restraint did not keep it in its proper place, and by doing so enable it to preserve that form which " served as a model for the altar chalice."

How the Corset should be made.

The corset should only have bones in the back and front, unless the person it is for has lost her proper proportions, for in that case the sides must be supported as well.

Coutil is, in my opinion, too stiff a material of which to make a corset ; satin, even cotton satin, is preferable, since we do not want armour ; the most suitable material is chamois leather. I am still speaking of women who are not too stout.

We shall come to this point of perfection, no doubt. There are already corsets of net for the summer, and corsets which can be enlarged as you like, and which follow the movements of breathing, thanks to the elastic sides with which they are provided ;

they are meant for weak and delicate women.

Short corsets are better than long ones, from every point of view, both for the sake of grace and comfort. If they are too high under the arms, they will make the shoulders appear too high, which is to be avoided. If they go down too low, they will elongate the body too much, the legs will appear shortened, and thus that happy harmony of proportion which constitutes true beauty will be destroyed. A corset which is short on the hips leaves perfect lissomeness of movement. Do not be indifferent to the dimensions of the corset. The shorter the corset is, too, the slighter the figure will be. Long stiff corsets make a post of the body, the same size at one end as at the other.

Do not let yourself be dominated by the fashion when it imposes those long sheath bodies which make you look like an automaton. Resist with all your might the dressmaker who wishes to force you into one.

If you have allowed yourself to be encased
in the hard cuirass, unlace two holes at the
top and two at the bottom, and lace the
middle so as not to squeeze you in the least.
Thanks to this artifice, you will regain, even
in this hideous corset, grace and ease enough
to enable you to wait patiently the altering
of this important part of dress.

The corset must always be absolutely
clean.   A soiled corset is strong evidence of
carelessness and lamentable want of neatness
in the wearer.   The corset should be preserved by a little petticoat body with short
sleeves (a *cache-corset*), which can be sent to
the wash the moment it begins to look
soiled.

A white corset is the nicest of all, no
matter what the material is made of.   I do
not much like blue, pink, or mauve corsets ;
they soil as quickly as the white, and are in
less good taste.   The grey or putty-coloured
corsets always look soiled or dirty-white
from the first.

The black corset, it cannot be denied, is economical. It has the advantage of not getting soiled, for it is easy to keep the white lining clean till the corset is quite worn-out. A black corset in good condition is certainly better than a white one that is soiled and worn.

The Legs.

The moment you perceive that a little child's legs are inclined to be crooked, take care not to allow him to walk. Leave him to himself on the carpet, where he can roll about as he likes, and the little legs will soon get straight again.

To avoid varicose veins, men should fasten the ends of their drawers so as not to make a ligature round their legs, and women should take care not to garter too tightly. They will, of course, not wear their garters below the knee—of which I shall speak presently.

Exercise develops the legs and enlarges

the calf. If you are not afraid of the ankle looking too clumsy, you will wear a high gaiter when going out walking.

Garters.

Garters should be a very carefully chosen part of dress. They may be simple; they must be irreproachable. I mean that they should always be clean and fresh, never ragged or shabby. I do not approve of garters all lace and ribbon, very smart or flowery. In America the garters do not match; a pair is composed of one yellow and the other black, or one yellow and the other blue, etc. One of the two is always yellow. It is said that this brings good luck. I do not know whether the yellow should be worn on the right leg or on the left. This dissimilarity is very ugly, and it is necessary to have a great deal of faith in the talismanic virtue of this yellow garter to commit knowingly this fault of taste.

There is an advantage, from the point of view of economy, as well as from that of refinement, in not buying cheap and common garters, which will not last, and will hold up the stockings very badly.

How to Fasten Stockings.

Everyone cannot bear a garter as tight as it should be. Their legs swell under pressure, and varicose veins form. In this case the stockings should be fastened to the stays by ribbons (suspenders). But accidents might happen; for if the ribbon, which must be well stretched to hold up the stocking, were to break, down comes the stocking over the heel! What a catastrophe! My advice is to wear at the same time a garter not at all tight, but sufficiently so to hold up the stocking, in case of accidents, until the damage can be repaired.

To wear the garter below the knee is against all rules of taste. The shape of the calf is compromised thereby, and deprived of the natural grace of its outline, which is thus voluntarily spoilt.

But, after all, it would be difficult to find any but an old peasant-woman who would wear her garter below the knee, and she only because the shortness of her stocking will not allow of anything else.

All women who wear long stockings have for some time been in the habit of gartering them above the knee; and it is only in out-of-the-way country parts that to do this, cords, tapes, and bits of string are sometimes used. The most humble servant-maid who is a little civilised buys elastic garters with buckles. Before ten years are over, the abusers of the garter of whom we have been speaking will, let us hope, have disappeared.

The Chemise.

If the chemise, the drawers, the little under-petticoat, and the slip-bodice could all be made to match, it would be in charm-

ingly good taste. They should in that case
all be of fine nainsouk or fine cambric, with
embroideries or valenciennes. The prettiest
chemise is cut out either round or heart-
shape. A ribbon run in tightens it a little
round the shoulders. It is also buttoned
on the shoulder. The neck and shoulders
are edged with valenciennes or a light
embroidery. The chemise must neither be
too wide nor too long. It should not fill up
needlessly either the stays or the drawers.

The Night Chemise.

Neither the flannel nor the linen which
has been worn by day should be kept on at
night. It is cleaner and more healthy to
change.

The night chemise should reach down
to the feet, and should have long sleeves.
It is trimmed with frills, embroideries, or
lace, and is finished off with a large collar,
falling to the shoulders in pleats. Ribbons
are sometimes put in at the collar and

I *

cuffs. It is, of course, made of washing
material.

After taking off your nightdress you
must, unless you change it every day, have
it aired as long as the bed—*i.e.*, for several
hours. After this put it into a bag and
hang it up.

Dressing in the Morning.

I have already said that it is best to
wash the face overnight, and not to expose
the skin to the air after it has been wet.
In the morning the face should be wiped
with a fine towel, and an entire bath taken,
followed by friction; or, if it is impossible
to do this every day, all indispensable
ablutions must be performed, every care
must be taken for necessary cleanliness,
without shrinking either from the trouble
this entails, for which one is so well rewarded, nor from the loss of time, for these
are moments well employed in the cause of
health.

The hair is then combed and arranged
tidily, but usually dressed later. All
depends, however, on the kind of life that
is led. Those who go out early in the
morning must have their hair dressed and
be armed *cap a pied* in good time. Those
who busy themselves in their households
must repair the disorder caused to their
attire by the work they have been doing
when this work is done. They must get
rid of the dust that may have settled on
face, neck, and hair.

Those who work in their households, as
well as those who only superintend them,
should, on first getting up, dress themselves,
with perfect neatness and care, as nicely as
possible. It is as well to change the undergarments—stockings, petticoats, etc.—as
well as the dress, when getting ready for
the afternoon, whether to remain at home
or to go out.

Undressing for the Night.

Many people prefer taking their bath at night; in any case, both night and morning the body demands ablutions to refresh and clean it. Under the heading "The Complexion" will be found the necessary directions for washing the face, which should be done at night. The hair should be well combed out, to free it from the dust of the day. For its arrangement at night, necessary hints will be found in the section on "The Hair." Men also should brush their hair; and if they will take my advice, they will wear no nightcap till they are at least sixty. A bandanna, or the head-gear of the *Roi d'Yvetot*, always gives them a slightly ridiculous aspect.

The Clothes we Take Off.

Never put up directly, neither in drawers nor in cupboards, any of the clothes you take off. Open them out, or hang them up in an airy place for at least an hour. Then, after having brushed and folded them, put them by.

The clothes which cannot be washed should be occasionally hung out in the air for a day, and turned inside out.

You may accuse me here of going into too great detail; but I can assure you that clothes which have been worn a long time, if care has not been taken to air them enough, or clothes that are shut up immediately after being taken off, contract an unpleasant savour.

It is most necessary to take precautions against such very disagreeable odours, so antagonistic to all refinement.

Saturating yourself with scent does not suffice to disguise them; you offend people with a delicate sense of smell, and you are immediately labelled.

Air as well as water, the heat of the fire as well as that of the sun, have disinfecting and purifying qualities which we ought to know how to use.

Part III.

—◦◊◦—

ADVICE AND RECIPES.

Feminine Diet: Nourishment.

IN order to avoid growing old (that bank-
ruptcy for the sex!), nourish yourself with
food, light, but nutritious and varied, according to the seasons. It will be found very
wholesome to take milk for one's first
breakfast. Eat little at the second, especially if you are going to do any kind of
work after it. The principal meal of Roman
soldiers and workmen took place in the
evening, after work was over. At the second
breakfast an egg and a vegetable ought to
suffice. Dine at six o'clock, or at seven at
the latest, and do not have too great a
number of dishes. Take a small cup

of milk and a light biscuit when you go to bed.

A diet too rich or too *recherché*, the abuse of butcher's meat, sauces, liqueurs, and old wines, are very bad for the complexion.

To obtain and to preserve a good colour, you should adopt a light diet, and eat meat once a day, and then in moderate quantity. Vegetables, on the contrary, may play a prominent part in the regimen. Some are more favourable than others to good-looks. In the fourteenth and fifteenth centuries soups were made of white chickweed, to clear the complexion. These soups were called "*soupes au roi*," because Odette de Champdivers, who nursed Charles VI., had conceived the idea of giving him the herb in this form as a remedy. White chickweed was also eaten as a salad; decoctions and infusions were likewise made of it, and were taken to clear the face from redness and flushings. This herb might well regain the place then given it among eatables, for it still retains all its virtues.

A rhymed proverb of the Renaissance recommends certain vegetables especially, saying that " spinach and leeks bring lilies to the cheeks."

To these may be added cucumbers, carrots, and tomatoes ; and many others, if not as good, are good. Gingerbread and rye-bread ought to have a foremost place among the foods preferred. A small slice of either between a second light breakfast and a moderate dinner will not overload the stomach.

Too much butter, bacon, fat, and oil in cooking, is to be deprecated, from the point of view of health as well as from that of the delicacy of the complexion. It is not necessary to exclude pastry absolutely, but only to admit it rarely : once a week at the most. Sugar should be used in modera-tion, and *bonbons* hardly ever. Acids are not all desirable. Preserves should not appear

upon the table every day. In very many
cases cheeses are altogether forbidden,
except Gruyère, which is considered a
purifier. Tea, coffee, and chocolate are
harmless, if they are used moderately. Milk
and lemonade are, on the other hand, excellent for the complexion. Wine should
be largely diluted—at least as much of the
same quantity of well-filtered water as of
wine.

If it were possible to swallow a glass of
hot water before the principal meal, the
complexion would be all the better. Mineral
and digestive waters are excellent for mixing
with wine.

Eat plenty of fruit: that is to say, eat
it often, every day at dessert. All fruits
are good, but some are better than others.
Use strawberries abundantly while they are
in season, unless indeed you have a tendency
to eczema. They purify the blood and the
liver, and are said to cure rheumatism and
gout, if their good effects are helped by a

severe diet. Shall I go so far as to say
that they cheer the spirits, as some affirm?
Cherries are also said to have the same
quality, and to cure "vesania," a disease
of the mind. Red currants are very refreshing, and so are plums. The peach,
that queen of fruits, is very good for the
stomach.

The apple is the most wholesome of all
fruits, and its good properties are innumerable; the orange is also to be specially
recommended.

It is said that the Baroness X——,
who was one of the beauties of the Court
of Louis Philippe, and who, at the age of
eighty, still had bright eyes and the complexion of a young girl, lived almost entirely
upon oranges during forty years; she had a
dozen oranges for breakfast, a dozen oranges
in the middle of the day, and a dozen
oranges, a slice of bread, and a glass of claret
for dinner.

I cannot say I advise such a diet, but

certainly the prettiest women are generally as frugal as camels in their food.

The Marquise de Crégny, who lived last century, and died at the age of nearly a hundred, only ate, for fifty years, vegetables stewed in chicken broth, and cooked fruit. She never drank anything but water, except during pregnancy, when the doctors made her take sweetened wine. In the last forty years of her life the water she drank was boiled, and had a little sugar-candy melted in it.

Several of my acquaintances who have exquisite complexions eat nothing but vegetables and cooked fruit all through Lent, and only drink water.

A group of pretty society women out-do even these; they are not satisfied with the abstinence imposed upon them for forty days, but go on fasting for two weeks after Easter, taking nothing but vegetables and fruit. They explain this extension of penitence by the necessity of counteracting

the effects of fish, which has so large a place
in the Lenten diet. The inhabitants of the
salt waves, when indulged in too freely,
bring out pimples on the purest complexions.
This is the reason why many women eat
fish sparingly at all times. Shell-fish, above
all, are to be looked upon with suspicion.

If you will follow the easy advice that
has been given here, the results obtained
will surprise you. Diet does far more for
health than doctors and drugs.

There can be no beauty without health.
Directly you feel a little out of sorts, a more
or less curtailed diet is generally the best.
If you feel unwell, give up at once the more
substantial foods and generous wines; the
hours of meals should be regulated, allowing
a sufficient time between each.

It is well to remember that that which
sustains life may also destroy it. To keep in
good health, it is necessary to know how to
restrain the appetite. In spring especially,
diet is of great importance; and a celebrated

practitioner told me that the "medical spring" begins at the end of January.

As one grows older the quantity of food should be reduced, and only very digestible dishes should be chosen. After sixty this becomes an absolute necessity.

The Life one should live.

A delightful old lady was asked by some young woman the secret of her pink-and-white colour, which she retained at an advanced age, while her contemporaries were sallow and faded; and in reply she sketched out a whole plan of life, which I will now give you:—

"Sitting up too late and sleeping too long in the morning spoil the complexion. Go to bed early and get up betimes; you will age less quickly, and will long retain your beauty. If, however, your position requires you to go into society, you must take care of yourself in this way: try to get a little sleep in the afternoon of the day on which you have to sit up late. When you come in, before going to bed plunge into a warm bath for a few moments; then take a cup of soup and half a glass of Malaga. You will go to sleep immediately, and you will remain asleep until you awaken naturally, which under such circumstances will not be till about ten o'clock. Then take a cold bath, sponging yourself all over; and have a light breakfast of *café-au-lait* and bread without butter."

The old lady added : " How necessary it is to go out as little as possible ! What an amount of precious time *fêtes* and parties make us lose before, during, and after them ! "

She continued : " Walking in the open air is very good for the complexion; but out-of-door sports must not be abused. While a daily walk of reasonable length is to be recommended, we must remember that the complexion will suffer if whole days are spent in playing lawn-tennis, croquet, etc.

Wear warm and light clothing, so as to keep your body always at an equal temperature. In winter keep the spine well protected; it is even more important than to protect the chest. Wear a silk handkerchief under the chemise if you don't like to wear flannel whilst you are young. In any case, though you may be only twenty years old, if you are delicate you should cover the spine with a strip of flannel—tied with a ribbon round the throat, and reaching to the loins. You need not be afraid of colds, bronchitis, or phthisis, if you take this slight precaution, which will not prevent your wearing a dress low in front, cut in a point or square. Do not wear your clothes too tight. To do so is against both the rules of health and real beauty. To compress the vital organs too much, congests the face. The hands swell and grow red, the whole appearance becomes stiff and awkward. Give yourself plenty of breathing-room, let your hand be at ease in your

glove, and let your foot have all the room
it wants in the shoe.

"Take a glass of mineral water occasionally, in the morning—either of Seidlitz,
Epsom, or Hunyadi Janos, etc. If your
complexion becomes muddy, doctor yourself
for three nights running, when you go
to bed, with a teaspoonful of an infusion
of powdered charcoal mixed with honey.
Follow it up with a light aperient.

"Iron and quinine have a disastrous effect
on the complexion. Alkalines with a little
arsenic are, on the other hand, excellent
for it.

"Sponge the body every day with cold
water when you are in good health. Live
in a healthy house; and in winter do not
allow the temperature of your bedroom to
fall below about 60° Fahrenheit. Work;
employ your time. Read, and take an
interest in the great and beautiful things of
nature and humanity. Activity of mind
and body keeps old age at a distance.

Avoid excitements and excessive luxury; do not allow your passions to master you.

"Be temperate, and your features will become refined. Greediness disfigures and coarsens the body. There is nothing like a rigid temperance in everything for keeping or obtaining beauty and freshness of complexion. Do not 'make up' your face while you are young, if you wish to preserve a pure colour in your old age. When the silver threads begin to streak your hair, do not have recourse to dyes, which only make it come out, or destroy its colour and silkiness. A beautiful white head of hair is a more becoming frame for the face at a certain age than locks as black as a raven's wing or blonde curls. It is better not to have too many heavily-scented flowers near you. 'Flowers,' remarked an old doctor to one of my prettiest aunts, 'are envious of the beauty of women, and are capable of injuring it.' This was a charming metaphor by which he tried to convince his lovely patient of the danger of keeping them too near her. Headaches, which are the consequence of doing so, are certainly not an embellishment.

"It is alleged that women of a certain age do well to practise gymnastic exercises. But this would be very unbecoming to them. If they want to use their arms, why should they not do household work, as was lately prescribed to a northern queen, who followed this sensible medical advice? With the hands protected by gloves, one can dust, brush, and sweep to one's heart's content. This is a sufficient and useful form of gymnastics, natural and healthy, and not ridiculous, like the former.

"There is no doubt that the body should be exercised and the limbs kept active. But, above all, we should be cheerful, or at least serene. As we advance in life, let us try to improve ourselves more and more, and to be kind and tolerant. A benevolent disposition and a certain calmness of mind are among the indispensable conditions for preserving good-looks.

"In mature age, let us put away all pretensions to juvenility. A dowager in a *décolletée* tulle dress, with nothing on her head, is hideous, almost odious. It is her part to wear heavy and rich materials; she should cover her head with a lace mantilla, and her thin shoulders should be draped.

" A grandmother dressed like her granddaughter, or even like her daughter, is a horrible sight.

" She should still, however, continue to love youth in others, to welcome it with pleasure, and to smile upon it.

" In short, it is stupid to be afraid of the coming years, and which will come all the same. Let us accept our age. An octogenarian who continues to take care of her person can still be beautiful, charming, beloved by her children and her friends, young and old."

Secrets of Beauty.

You must well understand the nature of your skin in order to keep your good-looks.

If you have a dry skin, you cannot treat it as you would an oily one. If it is a flabby one, it requires quite different treatment from a firm one. But, whatever it is, it is necessary to be on your guard against the cosmetics that are sold, which corrode and coarsen, and even roughen it with horrible little white pimples, which nothing can cure.

Spring, river, and rain water seem to me the first and best of all cosmetics, excellent for every skin. The rather oily juices of melon and of cucumber suit dry skins. Strawberry-juice is good for greasy skins. An infusion of lavender or of marjoram will give tone to a soft skin.

Nevertheless, one must not overdo such remedies. They should never be used daily, at the cost of losing their effect after a time.

All treatments should be interrupted for some days from time to time. Our bodies quickly become accustomed to medicaments of all kinds, which then cease to be efficacious.

A faded face (dry skins fade the soonest) will regain some freshness by using a lotion of which the following is the recipe. This lotion softens the epidermis :—

Boil some crumb of bread and roots of mallow in filtered rain-water. When the water is a little reduced, strain it through a clean white cloth, then add a good proportion of yolk of egg and some fresh cream. Stir it well, and perfume it with orange-flower-water.

This lotion has to be made fresh every time it is used. It does not do to apply it even the next day, as it will have turned sour.

Plantain-water is equally to be recommended.

Pretty Octogenarians.

An octogenarian, as I have said, can still be beautiful and charming. I have seen more than one example of good-looks lasting to an advanced age. At eighty-five the Maréchale Davoust, Princess of Eckmühl, the wife of the conqueror of Auerstadt, had still a queenly carriage, superb eyes, and the most lovely complexion in the world, so dazzling as to rival her admirable snow-white hair.

The Maréchale had never washed her face with anything but clear water. She kept a perfectly simple table, except on the days when she entertained, and even then she did not diverge from her usual temperate habits. She was generous, benevolent, and hospitable, although (or because) she was such a great lady, and these qualities had caused her to retain her charm and grace, so that her society was sought for to the last.

She had been one of the most lovely women of her day, but she had resisted the successes of her beauty. In her youth her thoughts were always set upon her absent lover, on the husband far from her side, on the hero ever exposed to danger. Age could neither alarm nor depress her valiant nature, though she had had to endure many sorrows, and years had but made of her a matron at once attractive and dignified. Her eyes and her brow reflected healthy thoughts only, and she wore the halo of a strong, virtuous, and loving woman.

Everyone has heard of her daughter, the Marquise de Blocqueville, whose literary talent sufficed to place her in the front rank. But the Marquise is, besides, one of the most attractive hostesses in Paris, although she, too, has left youth behind her. Endowed with infinite goodness, grace, and generosity, finding her own happiness in making that of others, in bringing out the good qualities, great or small, of those she

likes, her pure brow shows traces of the
most noble pre-occupations of the mind; and
although she has suffered, her smile is of
a very penetrating sweetness. Like her
mother, she wears her own white hair, lightly
powdered, which heightens her likeness to
the adorable women of the eighteenth
century.

The Marquise dresses with rare distinction, without, however, spending so much
as most women of her rank. Attractiveness is a womanly duty, even to the last.

In her delightful book of thoughts,
poetically entitled " Chrysanthemums," the
Marquise writes : " The coquetry of age is a
sacred coquetry ; it commands us to take
more pains with ourselves not to displease
than we take in youth to please." All
women of a certain age should follow the
example of Madame de Blocqueville, instead
of imitating the fashions of their grand-
daughters. " There comes a time," says
the Marquise further, " when every woman

should dress in *her* fashion, if she does not wish to lose the dignity of her age by following *the* fashion."

Here are all the secrets for remaining till the end beautiful and attractive to everyone.

OBESITY AND THINNESS.

Stout Women.

EXCESSIVE *embonpoint* is a disfigurement to the human body, and causes it to lose all grace of outline. A woman looks forward with dread to becoming stout, for she must say good-bye to the perfection of her profile, to the slimness of her figure, and to the grace of her appearance.

Some have indeed the courage to submit to the most severe regimen, to the hardest treatment, so as to preserve their beauty; and they do well, for a woman must absolutely be, remain, or become pretty.

J

An Empress of Austria, perceiving one day that her statuesque chin was getting double and her waist increasing in size, gave a cry of alarm. What! was she about to lose the slimness which made her look twenty years younger than she was, to carry herself no more with the air of a goddess treading the clouds? No, no; she would do anything in order to remain the most beautiful sovereign in Europe. She, the best horsewoman in the world, gave up riding, and took to long walks every day, in all weathers.

A little later it was a Queen of Italy who was threatened with the same disaster. But neither would she submit to losing her character of being a pretty woman; and at once she grasped the pointed alpenstock of mountain climbers to scale the highest peaks of her kingdom.

In earlier times Diane de Poitiers took a walk every day to preserve her beauty.

A woman who is too fat cannot take a

step without puffing like a grampus, and being in a bath of perspiration; she is as heavy as an elephant; her waist and the great circumference of her hips give her an appearance of vulgarity, however distinguished-looking she may have been by nature. Her hanging cheeks, her swollen eyelids, give her a repulsive countenance. She loses beauty, shape, and grace.

I would not sketch such a portrait, nor thus dwell upon the ugly effects of obesity, did I not wish to awaken the vanity of those women who have allowed themselves to grow too stout, and did I not know that with good will and courage it is possible to remedy the evil. I wish, before acting as a doctor, to hold up a mirror to them; and if I have been severe, it is only that I may the better persuade them to seek a cure for this annoying defect—a cure which is within reach of all.

How to Avoid Growing Stout.

Obesity can be avoided by never giving way to laziness, by occupying the mind, and keeping the body active. You must be less given to taking your ease and indulging in such lengthy repose under your eider-down, such prolonged dozing in comfortable arm-chairs. Did anyone ever see a peasant who had grown too fat?

In fact, when there is a tendency to grow stout it is necessary to live with a kind of Spartan frugality. But there are people whose greediness is even stronger than their vanity or than their desire for good health. They never dream of giving up good living, rich dishes, old wines, or highly-spiced cooking; and yet we see that the poor wretches who never dine with Lucullus are seldom disfigured by becoming too fat.

Rouse yourselves, ye unfortunate fat ones, for indeed I pity you! Labour till

you bring the sweat to your brow. Be of
some good in the world; for no one has the
right to be useless. Reduce your good
things in number; to-day have one dish the
less, to-morrow another. You can send the
unnecessary luxuries to some poor neigh-
bour. You will thus be charitable to two
people—to yourself, and to some miserable
being who has to look at every crust of
bread before eating it.

Take as your motto " Work and Frugality," and by these means you will save
yourself.

How to Grow Thin.

Exercise, even rather exaggerated exercise, is one of the most esteemed means of
bringing the body to reasonable proportions.

Even a certain amount of fatigue should
not be feared; for when one is tired, the
rapidity of breathing is increased, the
starchy tissues and sugar are consumed, and
therefore do not turn into fat. This once

admitted, the habits to be cultivated have
all been indicated. Tear yourself from sleep
and from your bed very early; be stirring
about from the first moment of the day.
Go to rest late, and set yourself to some
sustained intellectual work.

It is necessary that perfect sobriety and
a strict diet should go hand-in-hand with
exercise. Foods which make fat largely
should be avoided. Of this description are
those which contain starch and sugar,
especially starch (such as wheat, rye, oats,
rice, potatoes, tapioca, sago, etc.), which
quickly produce a very undesirable *embonpoint*.

Excuse odious comparisons, but just
consider the case of the cooped-up capon,
stuffed with food till it is smothered with
fat, and compare it with that of carnivorous
animals which have been left by man in a
wild state; these know neither idleness nor
excess, and they are always lean. Let any
of you ladies who are beginning to have

too majestic an appearance hearken to my warning call. Give up going to the confectioner's, avoid all cakes, all sweet things, and sugared knicknacks. Even bread should be parsimoniously dealt out to you, and preserved vegetables prohibited.

You must live upon lean meat, eggs, a milk diet, fresh vegetables, salads, mushrooms, fruits, etc. You are not to be pitied; you can still have a first-rate bill of fare. But you should partake very moderately of the things you are allowed to eat, and leave off while you still have some appetite. Drink very little, even at meals, and mix your wine with Vichy or Apollinaris; these waters help to expel the gas from the body, which is an advantage to people who are much, or even a little, too stout.

It is not true that coffee makes people thin; on the contrary, when it agrees with them, it makes them fat. This result is not so much due to its own nourishing properties as the fact that it is an excellent digestive.

It assists digestion, and makes it so complete
that no nourishing part of the food eaten
escapes assimilation; this powerful stimu-
lant dissolves everything that can nourish
or fatten. Tea has the same properties, but
in a less degree. Take courage, then, and
submit to work and to privation. Corpu-
lence ruins man's strength and woman's
beauty, and destroys the elegance of both.
Moreover, it impedes the breath, makes it
troublesome to move about, and diminishes
the strength of the muscles, the nervous
energy, and the agility and elasticity of the
limbs. The most piquant and *spirituelle*
faces become insignificant if outline and
features are lost in superfluous fat, and the
enlarged body loses the harmony that
Nature has given to the human form
divine.

Finally, over-fat people are most liable
to suffer from apoplexy and dropsy. "People
of full habit," said Hippocrates, "are more
subject to sudden death than those of spare

habit." Fat people hardly ever reach a very old age. Take heed, therefore, all you who love life!

Thin Women.

An angular form and a want of flesh that displays the skeleton under the skin are considered a disgrace in a woman, more especially as a bad complexion nearly always goes with them.

It requires courage to listen to the fun people make of a thin woman. "She is a stick!" "She is as flat as a board!" etc. etc. You must never imagine that, to be *distinguée*, it is necessary to be thin, though I have heard this asserted by some dried-up old ladies.

Excessive thinness is sometimes joined to an unpleasant temper—a fact I mention because it is curable. People of this temperament torment themselves; they are busybodies, plaguing themselves and everybody else; they are excitable, impatient, always fussing about. All feminine grace disappears in such an existence.

Fuss is not activity; but a well-ordered activity is advantageous to beauty, to health, to a wisely-regulated life.

A thin woman generally has a muddy complexion, because she is often—vulgarly, but truly, speaking—making bad blood. It is her own fault if she does not become pink and white, and rounded in form.

How to Acquire Flesh.

Thinness is often caused by too poor living—that is, by badly-chosen and insufficient food—and by over-fatigue, especially when brought on by prolonged brain-work and excessive anxiety. It is also promoted by a nervous and bilious temperament and a gloomy disposition.

"Laugh and grow fat." Cultivate peace of mind. Go to bed early, get up late, but keep regular hours. Do not overwork yourself; take moderate exercise when the

weather is fine. Take your meals punc-
tually ; you require a diet that is abundant
and wholesome, but without excess, composed chiefly of farinaceous foods, well
selected, of the best quality, easy to
digest and to assimilate—above all, bread,
thickened soups, tapioca and sago, Indian
sago, oatmeal, Carolina rice. Meat should
have a subordinate place in your diet, but
it should be of the best quality. Your early
breakfast should consist of *café-au-lait* or
chocolate; black coffee you should take
after luncheon, a glass of good old claret
after dinner, a cup of tea in the evening.
Lead a quiet life, with as few emotions as
possible ; amuse yourself in your own home.
Take tepid baths, and, above all, keep good-
tempered and cheerful. In this way you
will conquer your excessive thinness. A
slim woman with graceful lines may be
very attractive. A thin woman is ugly,
or at least uglier than she need be. A
proverb of the Ardennes affirms that

there is no such thing as a beautiful skin on bones.

Concerning Æsthetics—Rational Coquetry.

It is not enough to be a good wife and a good mother in order to retain the affections of your husband, the father of your children; you must also be an attractive and pleasant woman. It is sometimes easy to become pretty and agreeable to look at. Begin by choosing, in your dress, colours which suit your complexion and your hair; make the best of your feet by wearing becoming shoes; put on occasionally a wide open sleeve (in your summer *peignoirs*, for instance)—a sleeve which will allow a rounded white arm to be seen ; mark by a girdle the slenderness of your waist, instead of wearing shapeless garments; dress your hair so as to frame the face softly, and not to hide the shape of the head.

Instead of this, what does one often see ?

A woman who adores her husband, and yet never thinks of what will please him, who wears dresses of dark and gloomy colours, giving her a dull and sad appearance. She will stuff her feet into huge and common slippers, and always hide up her pretty arms, which may be so attractive. She appears in a shapeless dressing-gown, which makes her look all of a piece; twists up her hair, tidily enough perhaps, but without taste, so losing the best opportunity of enhancing her beauty.

Believe me that a certain amount of vanity is not only allowable, but that it is even our duty to make the best of ourselves in the eyes of the man we love. He will love us all the better, more warmly and faithfully. Is not this well worth the trouble? If we give up the battle, no matter how comfortable and cosy we make his home, he may be fascinated by someone else who is cleverer than we are. Perhaps he will remain faithful to us, his heart may still be ours, but duty only keeps him at our side. He must be made to feel attraction as well as duty, so that he should make no disadvantageous comparisons between us and another.

Many women may surpass the wife in beauty, but if the latter makes the most of her natural gifts, and knows how to enhance them by the care of her person and her dress, her husband will not be conscious of the fascinations of others.

It is a mistake to take no heed when the complexion becomes muddy, or when anything happens to diminish good-looks; a remedy should, on the contrary, be sought as quickly as possible. In fact, it is not wise to neglect our appearance, even for a moment, if we value our own happiness or that of our husband or children.

When I see a woman with her hair badly done, wearing a faded and ugly dress in her own home, I feel that it augurs badly for the future, even if the present is happy.

It is for the companion of our lives that we should keep all our pretty womanly ways; it is for him that we should try to look beautiful, cared-for, and sweet. Overcome your indolence, take outdoor exercise, or indoor if you have not time for long walks, and do not neglect baths and ablutions, which will help to preserve both beauty and health.

If you are intelligent, you can both keep and improve your good-looks. Add culture of the mind to that of the body. At the same time watch over the details of your household and look after your children. Those who would remain beautiful and beloved, must keep active in body, heart, and mind.

Lastly, remember that all the advice in this book is brought together in the hope of helping you to be happy; do not, therefore, despise any of it.

The Art of Growing Old Gracefully.

The secret of vanquishing old age is not to be afraid of it, nor to shrink from facing the advancing years.

It is, not to resort to absurd, stupid, and dangerous tricks, in the vain hope of retarding it.

It is, to give up a youthful attire, which only makes people look older when it does not suit them.

It is, to keep a kind heart for the young, to like them without being jealous of them.

It is, to retire from the struggle with dignity, not trying to rival your daughters.

It is, to surround oneself with true and gentle affection, which keep the heart green.

It is, to keep up our interest in the questions of the day; to take a delight in talking of great discoveries, of beautiful inventions; not to deny the progress of things, and not to try to make out that the old times were better than the new.

It is, to give advice with gentleness, and not to imagine that years have taught you everything.

It is, to be good and beneficent, in heart and word and deed.

It is, to take more pains than ever with your person. If you neglect any of the little habits of neatness, decrepitude will come on all the faster; and an old person who is careless and untidy presents a far more repulsive appearance than a young one, though such negligence is to be reprehended at all ages.

Finally, it is to wear handsome dresses, rich but simple, without pretension, comfortable, but not necessarily without grace.

Be assured that under these circumstances men and women may overcome old age, and be a pleasure to look at and to be with to the last. If it cannot be said of them that they are young, still less will they be called old, for they are old in years only, and have none of the infirmities of age.

Great Ladies of Society.

Do we not often hear So-and-so, the
Princess Z——, the Duchess X——, Mrs.
A——, or Mrs. B——, spoken of as young,
beautiful, and attractive women?

Suddenly you hear that they are fifty,
sixty years old; but you happen to have
seen them, and you cannot believe, any more
than can their admirers, that they are as old
as they are said to be.

These great ladies, whose whole delight
and happiness is their success in society,
have determined to keep young and beautiful, and they have succeeded up to a
certain point. They manage to look at
least fifteen years younger than they are.

Not for an instant have they neglected
the care of their beauty, submitting to anything to keep off the approach of age, to
preserve the least of their advantages intact,
or to acquire those obtainable by care and
effort.

Step by step they have struggled bitterly, every time that sickness, sorrow, or fatigue have attacked their beauty.

Bowing their heads for one moment to the storm, they have raised them again: they have battled, because for them it was a question of life and death. It was, from a worldly point of view, " to be or not to be," and they have succeeded in triumphing over time and nature.

Without going so far as to make sacrifices which are not compatible with the life of a good wife and mother, will you not also do your best, with the allowable means which I have pointed out, to retard old age and ugliness? It will be easier for you than for them to do so. The healthy activity in which you spend your days is all in your favour, while fashionable women are continually obliged to repair the ravages caused by their lives of pleasure and excitement.

They have sought to satisfy their self-love and vanity; your object is to remain the good fairy of the home, the delight of the eyes of him to whom you are entirely devoted.

The Secret of Looking Young.

" If you do not wish to grow old," said a charming old lady to her husband, when she saw him looking gloomy, " if you wish to keep always young, you must be amiable."

A darkened brow, a morose countenance, an unpleasant expression, what are these but a winter landscape ?

A serene face, a sweet expression, a kind and gentle look : these are like a day in spring, and the smile on the lips is a ray of sunshine.

Discontented people, you may notice, always look ten years older than they are. The face gets wrinkled by frowning, pouting causes the mouth to protrude disagreeably, and they rapidly grow old and ugly.

Compare with them a woman with a cheerful face; all her features are in their right place, her mouth curves delightfully, benevolence softens the expression of her eyes, and goodness beams from her smooth brow.

She is perhaps older than the ill-tempered woman whom you see beside her, but she will always look like her younger sister.

Grace of Movement.

Harmony must govern our movements if we wish to be graceful.

The stars in their courses are harmonious, but if they attempted to escape from the laws of attraction and gravitation, a terrible confusion would ensue in the universe. Discords, neither calculated nor resolved, destroy the harmony in music, and offend the ear. Examples might be employed indefinitely to show that harmony rules, or ought to rule, everything, from the procession of the stars to the movements of the smallest insect.

Some women have, in an extraordinary degree, the gift of unconscious harmony. I know some who choose their seats, their attitudes even, to suit their toilette, and they do so unconsciously. If they are dressed in a simple costume, they will lean against a piece of furniture severe in style, or will choose an oak chair which will be in perfect harmony with their appearance in their rather stiff tailor-made costume. They sit bolt upright in this chair which does not conduce to ease. If they are clothed in silk and lace, it is to the sofas covered with satin, to the plush ottomans, and the velvet easy-chairs that they will turn with a charming movement: careless indeed, but without awkwardness. Their bare shoulders will seem to caress the soft object against which they lean, and they will appear to sink into the deep cushions of their seat. They thus unconsciously make adorable *tableaux-vivants* and harmonious pictures.

It can never be the same with the stiff,

dry, angular woman who has not learned to be graceful, whose movements are sudden, abrupt, and full of awkwardness, because she does not know how to balance her body properly, which is the real secret of grace. Those who know how to walk and to hold themselves have this equilibrium. Nature may bestow this gift upon them; they have, at any rate, not lost it by bad habits, by not keeping a watch over themselves; or they have regained it by practice. This is the case with great actresses. Watch them moving on the stage: when their feet are in motion, the weight of the body is thrown upon the hips, and thus keeps its proper balance. All their movements are good, because they understand the laws of harmony. When the actress bows, she bends her body and raises it again with one quiet and equable movement.

You will never see her arm stretched out straight, imitating the horizontal line in the first position. If the arm has to be stretched

out, it is only in the second stage of the
gesture that it attains that position. It is
raised first, and then extended. If it was
at once stretched out, she would look like a
wooden doll. I am now going to point
out what is necessary in order to learn the
science of grace, which is not an affectation,
as might be feared, for it rests upon a
principle of Nature.

How to Walk.

If you are in the habit of stooping when
you walk, go about with your hands behind
your back when alone in your garden or
your own house. Children should be taught
to hold their shoulders well back ; and to
do this, they must be made to keep their
elbows close to their bodies. They will
then walk naturally, with the head up and
the chest thrown out. The back will be
straight and the shoulder-blades well in
their places ; the bust will be properly
curved, the entire weight of the body thrown

upon the hips, as it ought to be, to preserve its perfect balance. You must be careful to place the ball of the foot first on the ground, so as not to walk on your heels with the toes turned up—an ugly and vulgar habit, which makes the whole appearance ungainly, and entails unnecessary effort. Nature enables us to avoid this by providing us with an instep.

When we are going upstairs or climbing a hill, we often stoop and bend down our heads. But we should hold ourselves well up, for the sake of the lungs as well as of appearance.

Women who walk well by nature, or who have been taught to do so, like goddesses scarcely crush the flowers upon which they tread.

Grace of Form.

If you wish to remain slim, you must learn to hold yourself well. If women were more careful about their carriage, they

would keep their waists small and be less
corpulent than they often are by the time
they reach the age of thirty. The woman
who holds herself upright, and does not
bury her chin in her dress, but keeps her
shoulders back, thus naturally curves out
her chest, preserves the muscles firm and
well stretched, and the whole frame in good
shape. In this manner is avoided that
dreaded thickening which robs the figure of
all youthful elegance.

A well-balanced figure gives a queenly
carriage and the movements of a nymph.
Do not be afraid of looking too haughty.
If your eyes are sweet and your smile
pleasant, a slightly haughty air will not
deprive you of sympathy from others, but
rather the contrary.

I do not tell you to go so far as to hold
up your head, to stiffen yourself, and spread
your tail like a peacock; but to hold yourself up, as you are intended to do by
Nature, whether you are sitting, standing,

or walking. You will thus avoid looking like a bundle, and preserve the proper structure of your figure.

When you have to stoop or to bend, you will accomplish this with much more grace and flexibility than a woman who has allowed her back to become round, and spoilt her whole figure by neglecting her carriage.

Nature always punishes us if we violate her laws. She requires the human race to hold upright the body she has given it; she wishes man to raise up his head. If you allow yourself to be drawn down to the earth, you will lose all beauty of form.

Advice to a Stout Woman.

A stout woman should not wear a tailor-made dress. It marks the outline too decidedly, and throws every pound of flesh into relief.

She must deny herself bows and rosettes of ribbon at the waist, both back and front, as this adornment adds to its size. She ought not to wear short sleeves, as the upper part of her arm is sure to be too fat, and to look like a ham or a leg of mutton.

A ruffle round the throat will not suit her, nor a very high and tight collar. She ought to have her dress slightly open in a point in the front, or her collar a little turned back. A feather boa is the only one which will not shorten her neck too much.

Short basques will make her look ridiculously stout.

Wearing the hair low down will not be becoming to her. She ought to dress it high up on her head, without dragging it too tight; the front should not be plastered down. A certain carelessness in arranging her hair will be best for her, and she must not oil it too much.

Patterns with large flowers, and both large or small checks, must be avoided for her mantles and dresses. Stripes and plain materials, or small patterns in one colour, are all that she can allow herself, and she should wear dark shades.

Few jewels, no pearls round her throat, no earrings, and only as many rings as are indispensable.

Sleeves high on the shoulder and with tight cuffs must also be avoided, and she should not wear tight gloves.

Principles of Dressing.

The woman who pretends to be indifferent to her toilette is wanting in good sense. There is no doubt that it is an important question for us. The shape of one's garments, the colour and texture of the material of which they are made, have an importance that it is absurd to deny.

A badly-dressed woman is only half a woman, if her being so comes from indifference. Madame de Maintenon alleged that good taste was an indication of good sense.

She, too, it was who condemned those women who trim up common materials and

bedizen themselves with hideous things.
And how right she was! It is not by
sticking on a ribbon here and a flower there
that we can achieve elegance. Nothing
spoils a toilette as much, or makes it look
so ridiculous, as ornaments out of place. A
dress of inexpensive material can look well
if it is simple and unpretentious.

We should never follow the fashion of
wearing harsh and stiff stuffs. In skirts
they go into hard folds, and in bodices they
are hurtful both to the skin and the
complexion.

Woollen materials are only wearable
when they are soft to the eye and to the
touch. Stiff silks can never make pretty
dresses. Coloured silks of moderate prices
make charming costumes when they are
well cut and tastefully made up; but a
black silk must be of good quality, and
therefore a good price. You cannot wear
cheap black.

Handsome feathers are a great help to

good dressing, and last a long time. They are the best ornament for a bonnet. If you can only afford poor feathers, it is better to have none.

Stiff ribbons are very ugly trimming for a bonnet; it is worth while making a little sacrifice to obtain a soft and pretty one. Never add ornaments to your dress that you cannot replace if by accident they are spoilt, as their absence would be too evident.

A velvet dress is very useful if you have two or three other dressy gowns; but if worn too much, it becomes crushed and ugly.

Mixed woollen and cotton stuffs are not pretty, and are worth nothing. A material all wool is more than twice as good as a common one.

Fair women are mistaken in wearing light blue, which gives a livid hue to some complexions. A rich blue, on the other hand, suits them very well. A dark blue velvet is perhaps what brings out their good points best of all. Neutral tints are very unbecoming to them.

Brunettes with sallow complexions should avoid blue altogether. It will give them a greenish hue, or make them look tanned. Those who have a good colour may venture to wear it. Green is doubtful for them, unless the skin is very white; but it is extremely becoming to blondes, especially those with a pink colour.

Pale brunettes should affect those shades of red which heighten their beauty. Crimson may perhaps be admitted for fair women. Yellow is a splendid colour for a pale dark woman, especially by candle-light, as it is much less strong by night than by day: it harmonises with the olive colour of the skin, which it softens very much. The complexion takes from it a creamy tint, which blends wonderfully well with bright eyes and dark hair. People may say what they like, but yellow is very unbecoming to blondes.

No one should wear a low dress who has not a good neck and arms. Sharp shoulder-blades and pointed elbows are not pleasant to look at, and are best covered. But what are you to do if you are going to a ball or to the opera? Your dress may be cut low, but veil your neck and shoulders cleverly with tulle or lace, and do as much for your arms.

Neither should a very fat woman wear a low dress.

As freshness is the great requisite in a toilette, do not wear your smart ones in bad weather. Do your shopping and business in a last year's dress and bonnet, and keep your best clothes for occasions on which correct and handsome dresses are necessary.

It is ridiculous to have too great a number of toilettes at once. We know how short a time a fashion lasts, and it is unpleasant, and almost ridiculous, to be out of the fashion.

A morning gown is a necessity. It

K

ought to be very neat and appropriate, whatever else it is. You must have an indoor dress for the afternoon, a simple toilette for walking, and a more dressy costume for ceremonious visits. This is the least any woman can do with. A clever woman of slender means will turn her old smart dresses into indoor ones. I need not make for rich women a list of dresses for church, dinner, the opera, evening parties, concerts, balls, etc., or of the accessories they should have.

I shall restrict myself to saying that it is impossible to wear diamond earrings by day with a tailor-made dress, and that the details of each toilette should go well together, from the boots to the bonnet: for instance, a smart bonnet should not be worn with thick boots and a common dress; with a neat little costume, a simple and becoming little hat must be worn; with a velvet dress, a suitable bonnet, gloves, and mantle.

DIVERS COUNSELS.

Making-Up.

I can hardly expect my advice will be
of sufficient weight with all my readers to
make them give up the deplorable and unbecoming mania for painting themselves—a
mania which lowers womanly dignity at a
certain age, as much as it compromises
beauty in youth.

For those who will continue, in spite of
my protestations, to make up their faces, I
will at least explain how to put on rouge as
it was done in the eighteenth century.

"It should be put on in straight lines
under the eyes, for a layer of carmine
heightens their brilliancy; three other
layers lower down should be gently rounded
off, and be placed exactly between the nose
and ears, never reaching below the mouth."

This slight touch of rouge will not

altogether vulgarise the face, as so often happens when would-be improvements are foolishly overdone, and thus offend people of taste.

In the last century, when rouge was a necessity, and indicated a certain rank in women, the ladies of the Court made a serious study of how to put it on their faces in a refined manner.

These charming women would have been much prettier if they had kept their own delicate wild-rose colour. As to enamelling! I will only just mention it. An enamelled woman can neither smile nor cry, for fear of cracking the plaster with which her skin has been covered. Her head is like china, cold and expressionless, and her complexion by daylight is livid.

And if you ask me about whitening your skins, I would reply that to do this is even worse for them than rouging. In the name of good sense and good taste, let this be left out of your dressing-rooms altogether, for to look like a clown ought not to be an object of ambition.

Various Dyes.

I can give a description of some harmless dyes to those women who will not reconcile themselves to wearing their own grey or white hair.

Very strong tea dyes light hair which is becoming grey a tolerably good light chestnut.

Chicory, in a brown and oily paste, is also a dye for light hair. It should be prepared in a strong decoction.

Iron nails steeped in tea for fifteen days will make another dark dye.

The Romans used walnut-juice when silver threads began to appear. Persians dye theirs with henna, which they apply daily. The henna-leaves are powdered, and then formed into a sort of paste with water. This is rubbed on the hair, which is washed two hours later, by which time it has

become ruddy brown, the colour of old mahogany. If the operation is repeated the
next day, and indigo is added to the henna,
a superb black, like a raven's wing, will be
the result.

But I must repeat that even these
anodynes are injurious to the hair. They
make it dry, stiff, and brittle.

The dyes of which the base is lead or
silver are extremely dangerous. Not only
do they bring on baldness (very common in
our days, alas! with the fair sex), but they
bring on mischief in brain and eyesight.

Is it possible that anyone, knowing the
danger, will imperil not only their most
precious ornament, but also their intelligence and the most precious of all their
senses?

Turkish women have a dye which is
less dangerous than ours. It is composed
of the ashes of incense and mastic, blended
together with a perfumed oil.

The Greeks use another process, which

I will mention, because I fear that I cannot bring all the world over to my opinion, and because it is less dangerous than those of our hairdressers.

Take of sulphate of iron 2½ drachms, and of gall-nut 1½ ounces. Boil the gall-nut in 10 ounces of water, strained through a cloth. Add to the water the sulphate of iron, and boil again till it is reduced two-thirds. Perfume it with a few drops of scent, and keep it in a well-corked bottle. Apply it with a camel's-hair brush, and repeat several times.

Modes of Softening and Strengthening the Skin.

All the vaunted cosmetics for polishing and strengthening the skin will, believe me, be used in vain, and may even end by making it look leaden and flabby.

Bathing in cold water and friction are the only means that exist for making the flesh firm and the skin like marble. The shock given to the blood by cold water produces a vitality which makes the flesh firm, and naturally benefits the skin also. Friction removes little roughnesses from the skin. The down which sometimes comes on the arms will quickly disappear under the vigorous rubbing of the flesh-brush, or will at least remain below the surface.

A rough and dry skin can be improved by being rubbed with olive-oil scented with thyme. A flabby skin will be better for rubbings with essence of pimpernel mixed with essence of rose.

Nursing and after Nursing.

Do not believe that your bosom will lose its beauty and its form if you fulfil the sacred duties of a mother, and nourish the beloved child whom you have borne.

While you are nursing, you must, for the child's sake as well as your own, keep to a healthy, generous, and well-chosen diet, and afterwards still continue the same regimen for a certain time. With this care your bust will soon resume its proper shape and firmness. Nurse though you be, you may wear stays, but these should be special ones, suitable to your condition.

Do not, however, deny the fountain of life to the being to whom you owe it. And be assured that you will only keep younger and prettier for having submitted cheerfully to the law of Nature. If you hand over your maternal duties to a stranger, you will have to endure all sorts of evils and inconveniences, and you will only lose the beauty of your figure all the sooner.

TOILET-WATERS, PERFUMES, POMADES.

Toilet-Waters.

I DO not recommend the use of toilet-waters, or vinegar, either for the face or hands; but they may be useful for other parts of the body, as they give a tone to the skin.

The following are four recipes for eau de Cologne to suit various tastes :—

(1) Alcohol at 30° ... ... 1¾ pints.
    Essence of lemon ... ... 90 minims.
      „ of bergamot... ... 90 „
      „ of cedrat ... ... 45 „
      „ of lavender ... ... 23 grains.
      „ of neroline ... ... 8 „
      „ of roses ... ... 2 drops.

Shake the mixture well, strain it, and put it into bottles.

(2) Essence of lemon ... ... 2½ drachms.
      „ of cedrat ... ... 2½ „
      „ of bergamot ... 2½ „
      „ of fine lavender ... 2½ „

Essence of wallflower	...	$2\frac{1}{2}$ drachms.
" of rosemary	...	1 drachm.
" of thyme ...	...	$\frac{1}{4}$ "
Rectified alcohol ...	...	$3\frac{1}{2}$ pints.

Mix the essences with the alcohol, and strain through paper.

(3)
Essence of cedrat ...	...	$1\frac{1}{2}$ drachms.
" of bergamot	...	$1\frac{1}{2}$ "
" of neroline ...	...	15 minims.
" of lavender...	...	23 "
" of romarin ...	...	23 "
" of wallflower	...	1 drop.
" of China cinnamon ..	1 "
Tincture of musk amber	...	20 minims.
" of benzoin...	...	$1\frac{1}{2}$ drachms.
Alcohol at 90° ...	...	1 quart.

Dissolve the essences thoroughly in the alcohol, and strain.

(4) An exquisite recipe of the last century is :—

Essence of bergamot	...	$2\frac{1}{2}$ drachms.
" of orange ...	...	$2\frac{1}{2}$ "
" of lemon ...	...	75 minims.
" of cedrat ...	...	45 "
" of rosemary	...	15 "
Tincture of amber ...	...	75 "
" of benzoin...	...	75 "
Alcohol at 90° ...	...	$1\frac{3}{4}$ pints.

The alcohol used should always be the best, and

straining is indispensable. Eau de Cologne improves much by keeping. The firm of Jean Marie Farina keep it in barrels of different size, made of cedar-wood. Cedar preserves the perfume, and does not communicate its own.

Lavender-water can also be made at home. To make it, use:—

Essential oil of lavender	...	1 ounce.
Musk	...	1 drop.
Spirit of wine ...	...	1½ pints.

Put the three things into a quart bottle, and shake the mixture well for a long time. Leave it to settle for a few days, then shake it well again, and pour it into little bottles which must be hermetically sealed.

Or use :—

Refined essence of lavender	1 ounce.
Best brandy...	1¾ pints.

Mix a teaspoonful in a glass of water before using.

Use the same recipe for rosemary water, replacing the ounce of essential oil of lavender by 1 ounce of essential oil of rosemary.

As rosemary is mentioned, I must say something of the good qualities with which it is credited. It is asserted that the woman who uses it constantly, both as perfume and toilet-water, keeps young for ever. I will not answer for the truth of this assertion. Rosemary certainly belongs to the family of labiates, which are considered to be tonics and stimulants.

The pink has antiseptic qualities, which make it very useful as a toilet requisite. With its flowers can thus be made an exquisite toilet-water having a delicious perfume :—

Petals of pinks	... ...	8 ounces.
Alcohol at 90°	... ...	1 pint.

Infuse the petals in the alcohol for ten days, then strain through paper, and add 4 ounces of tincture of benzoin.

To make spirit of mint, take of :—

Refined essence of mint (called English essence of mint)...	2½ drachms.
Rectified alcohol at 90° ...	3 ounces.
8 or 10 drops mixed in a glass of water.	

N.B.—Never use brandy made from corn nor methylated spirit.

Toilet-Vinegars.

Never buy your toilet-vinegar ; make it yourself.

Acetic acid is sold under the name of vinegar, and is very hurtful to the skin, which it dries, corrodes, and wrinkles.

Take of :—

Eau de Cologne	... ...	3 ounces.
Tincture of benzoin	... ...	5 drachms.
Good plain Orleans vinegar		1¾ pints.

Pour into a big bottle or a jug the eau de Cologne and the tincture, and then the vinegar. Leave it for fifteen days, shaking the bottle every morning. Then strain it through paper. (Proper strainers can be obtained at any chemist's.)

Although these home-made vinegars are safer than the bought ones, even they should be used with caution. A few drops in a good quantity of water are enough to make it refreshing.

Beware of using white vinegar in any of your preparations.

Here is a recipe for a medicated vinegar as a remedy for rashes and pimples :—

Eau de mélisse	... ...	6½ drachms.
Spirit of mint	... ...	6 ,,
,, of sage	... ...	6 ,,
,, of rosemary	... ...	6 ,,
,, of lavender	... ...	6 ,,
Orleans vinegar	... ...	3½ pints.

Lavender vinegar is easy to make :—

Rose-water ...	... ...	6 drachms.
Spirits of lavender ...	...	1½ ounces.
Orleans vinegar	... ...	2¼ ,,

Aromatic vinegar is very inexpensive if you gather the herbs for yourself :—

Dry wormwood tops	...	10 drachms.
Rosemary ...	... ...	10 ,,
Sage... ...	... ...	10 ,,
Mint... ...	... ...	10 ,,
Garden rue ...	... ...	10 ,,
Cinnamon peel	... ...	75 minims.
Cloves ...	... ...	75 ,,
Pistachio nuts	... ...	75 ,,

Infuse for a fortnight in half a quart of alcohol, then add two quarts of white-wine vinegar ; strain through paper.

When flowers are in season, you can prepare exquisite flower-vinegars, for which the only expense is the vinegar :—

Good Orleans vinegar ...	1¾ pints.
Provence roses	1½ ounces.
Roses Cent Feuilles ...	1½ „
Flowers of jasmine	5 drachms.
„ of meadow-sweet ...	¾ ounce.
„ of melilot	¾ „
Leaves of lemon - scented verbena	5 drachms.

If, instead of fresh, dried flowers are used, a quart and a half of vinegar will be required. It is left to infuse for a month, and then strained.

For rose-vinegar :—

Dried petals of red roses ...	3 ounces.
Orleans vinegar	1¾ pints.

Eight days of infusion will be sufficient ; but the large-necked bottle into which the petals and the vinegar have been poured, must be well shaken, and the leaves well squeezed when the vinegar is poured off. Leave it to stand for about a couple of days, then strain.

All flower-vinegars can be made with 3 ounces of dried petals or flower-tops and

1 quart of vinegar. Mignonette is the sweetest of them all.

Virgin Milk.

To make virgin milk take :—

Powdered benzoin ...	...	1½ ounces.
Alcohol at 90° ...	...	¾ pint.
Good Orleans vinegar	...	¾ ,,

Put all into a bottle, and shake every morning. After fifteen days' mixing, strain through paper.

N.B.—It is necessary to blend the powdered benzoin with a small quantity of the alcohol and vinegar mixed, so as to make a light-coloured liquid, then add the remainder, stirring all the time, and pour into a bottle.

Perfumes : Their Antiquity.

Perfumes were held in high esteem among the ancients. In Egypt they were used even to excess; scents, more or less sweet, impregnated the persons and clothes, the tombs and houses of the people of that country; and at festivals the gutters ran with perfumed waters.

Did not the Shulamite plunge her fingers into the precious myrrh before hurrying to meet her spouse? The entire Bible is fragrant with nard and dittony; and the whole of the East has preserved this love of perfumes.

The Greeks had a scent for each part of the body: marjoram for the hair, apple for the hand, serpolet for the throat and knees, etc.; an infusion of vine-leaves was also highly esteemed by them.

This mixture of odours could not have been very pleasant. The ancients found out the use of the vaporiser before we did. The gilded youth of Athens used to let loose, above the festive board, doves which had been bathed in different scents, and which, hovering aloft, rained from their wings delicious perfumes over the guests.

At Rome the slaves filled their mouths

with sweet-smelling waters, and blew them
in showers over the hair of their mistresses.

The Romans, especially the ladies,
carried the habit of scenting themselves
and of living in the midst of strong perfumes so far that Plautus exclaimed:

"By Pollux! the only woman who
smells sweet is certainly the one who is not
scented at all!"

Amber and verbena were favourite perfumes at the end of the Middle Ages. In
the thirteenth century women hung up with
their dresses certain kinds of apples, which
impregnated the presses with a very delicate
odour.

The favourites of Henri III. adored
neroline and frangipani. *La belle Gabrielle*,
who reproached the Bearnese for their
liking for leeks, loved iris-root and orange-
flower. Anne of Austria had her cosmetics
scented with vanilla, and the Pompadour
was perfumed with rose and jasmine.

The Choice of Perfumes.

Scents may be used in moderation from the point of view of hygiene, on account of their stimulating and refreshing properties, but both health and good taste forbid their being over-done. They are not without effect upon the constitution and good-looks, especially, it is said, those made from lavender, lemon, roses, violets, and benzoin.

They are also supposed to have a certain effect upon the mind. Musk produces sensitiveness; geranium tenderness; benzoin dreaminess; dark-blue violets predispose to piety; white ones facilitate digestion. It is also asserted that a woman who likes the smell of lemon-scented verbena ought to cultivate the fine arts; for by this choice of perfume she reveals her artistic nature.

Without being over-scented, which is a mistake, it is well to perfume your linen and all your garments with a light and delicate odour—of one kind only—from head to foot. This enhances your attractions.

I repeat that every woman should reject a mixture of scents. She should choose a perfume, and keep to it. All her belongings, her books, her note-paper, her boudoir, the cushions of her carriage (in the eighteenth century they used to be stuffed with sweet-scented herbs, called " *herbes de Montpellier* "), her clothes, the smallest things she uses, should give out the same sweet fragrance.

It remains to choose that scent. A great lady wrote : " Satan smells of sulphur, and I smell of orris-root." She could not have chosen a more exquisite odour. Some people, in love with the last century, choose *peau d' Espagne*.

I consider it a mistake to look upon Russia leather as a scent.

Some women are satisfied with the aroma that their rose-wood wardrobes communicate to their clothes.

Others only use the scent of the fresh flowers and herbs that are in season. They begin with violets, roses, mignonette, etc., with which they fill in turn their drawers, their pockets (when the dresses are put away), muslin sachets, etc. etc. The perfume communicated by these fresh flowers and herbs, which fade and die where they are placed, would no doubt be very fugitive, but is extremely pleasant. The same people prepare flowers of melilot, meadow-sweet, and aspernla, dried in the shade, for winter use, and simply fill muslin bags with them, and place them about among their things. When they pass you by, they remind you of meadows full of flowers.

Our ancestors preferred pot-pourri among scents. They filled their sachets with it, so we give recipes for those who like it :—

(1) Rose leaves dried, or
    Powdered orris-root   ...   ... 1,500 parts.
    Powdered bergamot peel   ...   250 ,,
    Cloves and cinnamon ...   ...   150 ,,

Orange flowers and clusters of dried acacia flowers		... 250 parts.	
Powdered starch	...	... 1,500	"

	Powdered orris-root	...	...	500	"
(2)	Powdered orris-root	...	...	500	"
	Lavender	...	...	50	"
	Benzoin...	...	...	25	"
	Sandal citrine ...	...	...	25	"
	Orange peel	...	...	25	"
	Tonquin beans ...	...	...	10	"
	Cloves ...	...	...	10	"
	Cinnamon	...	...	10	"

Mix very carefully. The powders need not be very fine, and if they are not to be bought, it is easy enough to pound them for oneself.

	Florence orris-root powdered	...	750 parts.
(3)	Florence orris-root powdered	...	750 parts.
	Rosewood	... ...	165 "
	Calamus	... ...	250 "
	Sandal citrine ...	... ...	125 "
	Benzoin...	... ...	155 "
	Cloves ...	... ...	15 "
	Cinnamon	... ...	31 "

Modern perfumery, aided by chemistry, has invented delightful perfumes, among which it is easy to make a good choice. A refined woman will always reject odours which are too strong or too penetrating. Hers will

be sweet, light, and delicate, and will please
without being overpowering.

Sachets.

Sachets are very easily prepared.   You
have simply to sprinkle, more or less abundantly, square pieces of cotton-wool with
the perfumed powder you like best.
These squares are sewn up in muslin, which
is trimmed with lace.   Another way is to
put the powder into little bags of cambric
or thin silk, and to prettily tie them up
with ribbons to match.

Sachets for gloves, laces, handkerchiefs,
and stockings are as easily made.   They
have only to be larger, and trimmed as
prettily as possible.   These large squares of
wadded silk are simply doubled, and fastened
with ribbons.

Many refined women have their drawers
and the shelves of their wardrobes lined with
a thin satin quilt, of a delicate colour,
wadded with scented cotton-wool, held in

with rosettes of ribbon, forming in reality a very large sachet.

All their odds and ends of different materials, and their linen, lie thus upon beds of perfumed satin. Laces, handkerchiefs, and gloves are enclosed in delicately-scented sachets. Bonnet-boxes are impregnated with sweet fragrance; dresses, costumes, skirts, and mantles are hung up in wardrobes and cupboards among bags which give out a delicious odour. Everywhere the one favourite scent is introduced: in the hems of dresses, in the folds of sleeves, at the collars, and in the stays. The woman is entirely enveloped in it.

You can perceive her presence before you see her. You know by the fragrance of her note-paper whom the letter is from before you recognise the handwriting. If she lends you a book, its perfume is a standing reproach to you, if you have not returned it

Cold Cream.

Cold cream :—

Oil of sweet almonds	1½ ounces.
White wax	2½ drachms.
Spermaceti	2½ „

Mix these ingredients quite smoothly. Then add :—

Rose water	5 drachms.
Tincture of benzoin	75 minims.
Tincture of amber	30 „

I ought to say the wax and spermaceti should be melted, to mix with the oil.

Cucumber Cream.

Cut up into little pieces a pound of peeled cucumber, with the seeds taken out. Add as much of the flesh of melon, prepared in the same manner, and a pound of clarified lard and half a pint of milk. Let it simmer in a *bain-marie* for ten hours, without allowing it to boil. Squeeze it through a sieve with a cloth over it, leaving it to drip through and to congeal. Then wash the cream several times till the water runs clear. Wring it well in a cloth, and keep it in little pots. Here is another recipe:—

Axunge...	...	...	...	1 part.
Cucumber juice...		...	...	3 parts.

Mix well 1 part of cucumber juice with the whole of the axunge, which should be softened first. When you have beaten them well together for two hours, let it stand till the next day. Then let the liquid run out, and put another part of the cucumber juice into the ointment. Repeat as before. Do the same a third time, to use up what is left of the juice. Melt the ointment for five or six hours over a gentle fire, to let all the water evaporate. It must be often stirred to obtain this result. To make it light and smooth, the ointment is again beaten up, and then poured into pots.

Glycerine.

We have already said that glycerine does not suit every skin. You can soon find out whether it suits yours or not ; if it makes it red, do not use it.

Even if it does agree with you, it should not be used by itself.   Having the property of absorbing water, it uses up the moisture which the skin requires ; it is for this reason that the latter, especially with some people, gets red and irritable when they use glycerine.

Glycerine should therefore be diluted, and even more than diluted, with eau de Cologne : equal parts of glycerine, soft water, and eau de Cologne should be used.

Soaps.

If the face must be occasionally soaped, you should at least be careful to wash it afterwards two or three times with clear tepid water, and only use very pure white soap. Soaps are often scented in order to conceal the smell left in them from being badly made ; and the colours with which they are tinted, especially green and pink, are very injurious to complexion and health.

Do not forget that soap has a tendency to dry the skin and to stop up the pores. If it were possible to make our own soap, it would probably be much less hurtful. It is at least easy to improve it. Cut up a pound of white soap, and put it in an earthenware pot, add a little water, and place it before the fire. When the soap begins to soften, mix it with oatmeal into a thick paste. Melt it again, put it into shapes, and before it is quite cold make it into squares and balls.

In this manner all little ends of soap can be utilised, which would otherwise be wasted; they can at all events be used in the kitchen. Dissolve half a cupful of bits of soap in a cupful of water, and proceed as above.

The moulds should be greased before the soap is poured into them.

Face Powder.

The powder you buy is oftentimes hurtful to the skin. If we could make it for ourselves, not only would it be harmless, but very useful in those instances when, as I have already mentioned, it is necessary to use it.

It is quite easy to make, in the following manner :—

Take a new earthenware pot and fill it with six quarts of water and 2½ lbs. of rice; leave the rice to soak for twenty-four hours, and then pour the water off. Put the same quantity of water over the rice for three days running. After the three immersions, each lasting twenty-four hours, drain the rice over a new hair-sieve kept for the purpose. Expose it to the air in a safe place, on a clean white cloth. As soon as it is dry, pound it quite fine with a pestle in a very clean marble mortar with a cover. Then strain it through a fine white cloth placed carefully over the pot which is to hold it, and which ought to be provided with a tight-fitting cover. This powder is better without perfume.

If you run short of home-made powder, you can replace it safely by oatmeal-flour, of which you must take very little at a time on your puff.

If you buy your rice-powder, be careful not to choose it perfumed with orris-root, should your skin be inclined to be irritable.

You should never leave your puffs lying about; they should be kept in separate clean china boxes.

How to Perfume Soaps.

The soaps for which we have given recipes may be perfumed with good scents.

When the preparation is taken off the fire, pour in the scent, stirring it well before putting it into the moulds.

A soap scented with raspberry juice is perfectly delicious. For jasmine-scented soap, melt at the same time as the soap some ointment perfumed with this delightful flower. Essence of rose is very good to use in the same way.

Part IV.

—◦✦◦—

LITTLE HINTS.

How to Take Care of Jewellery.

Pearls.—If pearls are shut up with a
piece of ash-tree root, it prevents them losing
their colour.   Should wiseacres laugh at this
recipe, let them laugh, and believe the experience transmitted in old families from
generation to generation.   This precaution
will prevent them even from growing dim,
and is well worth knowing for those who
possess finely-shaped pearls of fine quality,
which might perish at the end of a hundred
years.

It is well to take an experienced con-
noisseur with you when you buy coloured

pearls, as they are easily imitated. The beauty and "skin" of the real pink pearl is evident to the most superficial observer.

Pink pearls set with white ones and diamonds form the most beautiful of all ornaments. The pink pearl of the Bahamas looks at first sight something the colour of pink coral, but is of a softer shade. It is not only lustrous, but its velvety surface has also charming iridescent effects.

The value of a pearl depends on its shape, size, "skin," and shade of colour. When it is round, it is called button-shaped; when irregular, *baroque*.

The happy possessor of a row of pearls the size of wild cherries may be interested to know that in the seventeenth century they went by the name of "*esclavage de perles*," and that the knots of diamonds sometimes suspended from it were called "*boute en train*."

Pearls are said to foretell tears. But women of the people, who do not possess a

L

single one, weep as much as the duchesses
whose jewel-cases are filled with these most
beautiful of feminine ornaments.

Diamonds.—Diamonds should be brushed
in a lather of soap, and rubbed afterwards
very carefully with eau de Cologne. Diamonds skaken in a bag of bran acquire
extreme brilliancy.

To discover whether a diamond is real,
make a hole in a card with a needle, and
look at the card through the stone. If it
is false, you will see two holes in the card;
if it is real, only one. Or, again, put the
gem on your finger, and look through the
stone with a lens; if it is false, you will see
the grain of the finger perfectly well, but
it will not be visible if the diamond is real.
The setting cannot be seen through a real
stone, but it can be seen quite clearly
through a false one.

Gems.— Cut stones should never be
wiped after they are washed. A soft brush
dipped in a lather of white soap should be

used to clean them. They should then be rinsed, and put on their faces in sawdust till they are quite dry. Sawdust of boxwood is the best.

Gold Jewels.—Gold ornaments should be washed in soap and water, and well rinsed afterwards ; they should be left in sawdust for some time, and when they are quite dry, rubbed well with chamois leather.

Opals.—Russian superstition has caused this many-coloured gem to be looked upon as a fatal stone. But mediæval alchemists did not agree with the subjects of the Czar about this. They maintained that the opal renewed affection, and kept the wearers from all evil, from all contagious germs, and that it also preserved them from syncope and all diseases of the heart. The Orientals allege that it is sentient, and that it changes colour according to the emotions of its wearers, flushing with pleasure in the presence of those they love, and paling before their enemies.

"The ancients," says Buffon, "held the opal in high repute," for its beauty chiefly. Charming things have been said about its varying tints. "Its light is softer than that of the dawn." "It might be said that a ray of rose-coloured light lies captive under its pale surface." It has been called the "tear-drop of the moon." It has been dedicated to the month of October, and those who are born in that month should prefer it to all other gems.

I might say much more about it, but I am forgetting that my object was simply to say how to restore its polish when it has been scratched and dimmed by wear. Rub it well with oxide of tin, or with damp putty spread on chamois leather, and finish with chalk, powdered and sifted, also spread on chamois leather and damped. Then wash the opal in water with a soft brush. If you are very careful, you can do all this without taking the stone out of its setting.

Silver Jewellery.—Filigree silver can be cleaned in various ways when it has become black and dull. It should be first washed in potash water, not too strong, and well rinsed. The objects should then be immersed in the following solution :—Salt one part, alum one part, saltpetre two parts, water four parts. They should not be left in this for more than five minutes, then rinsed in cold water, and wiped with a chamois leather.

Or they can be washed in hot water with a brush dipped in ammonia and green soap, then steeped in boiling water and dried in sawdust. They should always be put by wrapped in silver-paper.

Oxidised silver should be steeped in a solution of sulphuric acid one part, and of water forty parts.

Silver ornaments can also be cleaned by being rubbed with a slice of lemon and rinsed in cold water, then washed in a lather of soap and again rinsed, this time in hot water; dry them with a soft cloth, and polish with chamois leather.

Nickel and silver are kept bright by being rubbed with flannel dipped in ammonia. Tarnished amber should be rubbed with powdered chalk wet with water, then with a little olive-oil on flannel, till the polish has reappeared.

Ivory can be whitened with a solution of peroxide of hydrogen. Letting it stand in spirits of turpentine in the sunshine will also have a good result. A simple way of cleaning ivory is with bicarbonate of soda; rub it with a brush wet with hot water and dipped in the soda.

How to Take Care of Furs, Feathers, and Woollen Things.

Many things and substances are highly spoken of as preservatives against insects.

Pliny relates that the Romans used lemon to keep moths and their grubs from their woollen garments.

Nowadays some people use horse-chestnuts, others cloves, others walnut-leaves, others again kitchen salt, to keep this destructive insect from furs, feathers, and woollens; they vaunt the efficacy of these remedies, transmitted from one generation to another.

Generally, however, cedar - shavings, pepper, and large lumps of camphor (if powdered, it evaporates too quickly) are unanimously considered the best preservatives.

Whatever you prefer to use, you must be careful to shake, beat, and brush the fur the wrong way up, as well as everything you are putting away, when the season for wearing them is over. Sprinkle them then with pepper, and scatter pieces of camphor, or anything else of that kind you like, among them; pack them, well sewn up, in clean linen, and put them into a well-dusted case, into which you should also scatter some of the same disinfectant.

Cigar-boxes are the best receptacles that you can choose for your feathers when you are not wearing them.

If you have trunks of cedar-wood, or cupboards lined with it, you will find it quite sufficient simply to shake and brush your things before putting them away.

There are yet other preventives against moths. A liquid may be made by mixing half a pint of alcohol with the same quantity of spirits of turpentine and 65 grammes of camphor; it should be kept in a stone bottle, and well shaken before used. When you are putting away your winter clothes, soak some pieces of blotting-paper in the liquid, and scatter them about in the cases; after the things have been wrapped up in linen, put a layer of the paper under the things, and others over them and at the sides.

Another plan is to cover an old brandy-barrel with pleated cretonne trimmed with brown guipure. Wrap up your furs and best woollen things in linen, and put them into the barrel; it will not look amiss standing in the corner of your dressing-room, with a pretty plant on top of it, and is the safest place possible for your things at the dangerous time.

If you have neither cedar-boxes nor barrels, it will be sufficient to sew up your winter garments in linen bags, taking the same precautions, and then hanging them up in a dark cupboard.

Dark furs are cleaned by rubbing them the reverse way with warm bran, and light ones with magnesia.

How to Clean Lace.

Many ladies have their valuable point-lace washed before their own eyes whenever it is absolutely necessary, for good lace should be washed as seldom as possible. It is, however, easily cleaned. Make a lather with hot soft water and glycerine soap. Roll the lace on a glass bottle covered with

L *

a strip of fine linen, and leave it in the lather for twelve hours. Repeat this three times; then rinse it slightly by dipping the bottle in clear soft water, taking it out almost immediately. The soap which is left in serves to give a little stiffness to the lace when it is ironed. Each point must be pinned down before ironing it, which should always be done on the wrong side, with muslin over it. When it is done, all the flowers which have been flattened should be raised with an ivory stiletto.

Lace can also be cleaned by being put out in the sun in a basin of soapy water. It is then dried on a napkin, the points being pinned out as before, and very gently rubbed with a soft sponge dipped in a lather of glycerine soap; when one side is clean, do the other in the same way, and then rinse the lace in clear water with a little alum in it, to take out the soap; sponge it with a little rice-water before ironing it, and raise the flowers as above. If lace is not very much soiled, it can be cleaned by rubbing it very gently with bread-crumbs.

Blonde lace should boil for an hour in water with a little blue in it; this should be repeated twice in fresh water, and the third time the blue should be left out. It should not be rinsed. The blonde should be put into gum mixed with a little brandy and alum, then it is lightly sprinkled with sulphur, and ironed while it is damp.

Valenciennes should be rolled up in a convenient-sized packet, then sewn in a bag of fine white linen, and soaked for twelve hours in olive-oil, and boiled for a quarter of an hour in water in which a little white soap is cut up. Rinse it well, dip the bag in a thin rice-water, then unsew it, and pin the Valenciennes out flat, to let it dry. Iron it with muslin over it.

Black lace should also be folded up so as to form a small lengthy packet (which should be kept together by being well tied up with strong cotton), and then dipped

into beer.   Rub it in your hands, but very
gently, to clean it.   Squeeze it so as to get
the beer out, but do not wring it, and roll
it up in a cloth.   Iron it when it is more
or less damp, according to the amount of
stiffening that you want, placing it right
side upwards upon a thick blanket, and
covering it with muslin to prevent it looking
shiny.

When you put away dresses trimmed
with lace, cover up the lace with silver-
paper.

To clean silver lace or braid, enclose
them in a linen bag, plunge the bag in a
pint of water to which 2 ounces of soap
has been added, and boil;   then rinse it out
in fresh water.   Apply a little spirits of
wine to the parts that are tarnished.

How to Clean and Wash Woollen Materials.

Pink cashmere should be cleaned in a
cold lather.   Do not try putting any colour-
ing into the water; you will spoil the stuff.

Rinse it well in cold water, and dry indoors in a subdued light.

For cleaning serge, use a strong decoction of the root of soapwort, which will make it very white and soft to the touch. Soap hardens materials, and always makes them a little yellow.

Knitted and crocheted garments should be washed as follows:—Cut up a pound of soap into small pieces, and melt it till it is as thin as jelly; when cold, beat it with your hand, and add three spoonfuls of grated hartshorn. Wash the things in this liquid, and rinse them well in cold water.

Plunge them into salt-and-water to fix the colour, if they are coloured. Put them in a bundle before the fire, and shake them frequently to dry them; never spread them out for this purpose.

If you want to refresh a faded black cashmere, rub each breadth separately with a sponge dipped in equal parts of alcohol and ammonia diluted in a little hot water.

Merinos and cashmeres should be washed in tepid water with some potato grated in it, and well rinsed in fresh spring-water. They should not be wrung out, but spread out singly on a rope, where they can drip till they are two-thirds dry, and then ironed.

Black cashmere can also be washed in Panama-water (that is to say, water in which Panama wood has been boiled), ivy-water (prepared in the same way), or ox-gall; this last is also very good for green cashmere.

Here is another way of cleaning black cashmere :—Pick it to pieces, carefully taking out all the threads, cover the stains with dry soap. Put 6 ounces of mustard-flour in six quarts of boiling water, and allow it to boil up for two minutes. Strain it through a cloth, and let it cool till you can bear your hand in it. Put the stuff into an earthenware crock, and pour the mustard-water over it. Soap carefully, especially where it is stained, rinse it several times till the water runs clear, and stretch the material on a rope. When it is quite dry, cover it with a damp cloth, and iron it.

Coloured flannels should be washed in a warm lather, but never rubbed with soap. Shake them well, so as to get the water out as much as possible, and hang them up to dry.

Blue flannel must be washed in bran-water without soap; to preserve the colour, throw a handful of salt into the water it is rinsed in.

The juice of potatoes will remove mud-stains from woollen materials.

The white woollen *fichus* in Russian or Pyrenean wool, which are so useful in winter, can also be easily washed at home. Prepare a lather by boiling good white soap in soft water, which must be beaten continually while the soap is dissolving; then plunge the *fichu* into it, after having soaked it in clear tepid water. Squeeze without rubbing it, and repeat a second time; but this is not all. Dilute well two spoonfuls of powdered gum

arabic in rather less than a quart of luke-
warm water.   When the liquid is thick, dip
the *fichu* in, and squeeze it with your hands
several times.   Wring it out first in your
hands, and then in white napkins.   Dry the
fichu by stretching it out and fastening it
along the edges on a cloth, and covering it
with another.

How to Clean Silks.

Silks can be very well cleaned if carefully done.   Mix well together 12 drachms
of honey, the same quantity of soft soap,
and $\frac{13}{16}$ths of a quart of brandy.   When
the dress is unpicked and spread on a table,
brush it well with the mixture.   Rinse
twice, and a third time in a tub of water in
which 15 drachms of gum have been melted.
Hang up to dry without wringing, and then
iron it on the wrong side.

Another recipe :—Grate five potatoes in
some clear fresh water.   If your silk is a
thin one, cut up the potatoes instead of

grating them, and in any case do not forget
to wash them well before using. Leave
the water to stand for forty-eight hours, and
then strain it. Dip the silk into it several
times, taking care not to crush it; spread
it on a table, and dry it well with a clean
cloth on both sides. Iron on the wrong
side. If the silk has any grease-stains upon
it, they must be taken out first, either with
chalk, or with magnesia and ether, or with
yolk of egg and water.

White brocade should be cleaned with
bread-crumbs; plain white silk (not satin)
as follows :—Dissolve some soft soap in
water as hot as you can bear it. Rub the
silk between your hands in this soapy
water, giving the stains extra attention, and
rinse in tepid water. To dry, spread it out
pinned on a cloth.

How to Clean Velvet.

If you have a good lady's-maid, you can
easily get her to renew your worn, stained,

or shabby velvet garments. It is necessary to unpick them, whatever they may be, so as to clean each breadth or piece separately.

Heat a thick plate of copper of suitable size ; when it is very hot, put on it a cloth folded several times, and damped in boiling water. Then spread the velvet on it right side up, and do not be surprised to see a very thick black steam rising from it. At this moment pass, very lightly, a soft brush over the velvet. Take it off, and dry it by stretching it out on a table ; when dry, it will be as good as new. If you are not going to use it at once, wrap it up in silver-paper.

When velvet is crushed and flattened, it should be held stretched over boiling water, with the wrong side exposed to the steam, and then brushed up the reverse way.

Before putting away dresses and garments of all kinds made of velvet or plush, they should be well dusted. To do this, shake very fine dry sand on them, and brush them till the last grain of sand has disappeared. To take off mud-stains, brush with a soft brush dipped in gall diluted with some nearly boiling water, to which a little spirits of wine has been added; repeat if necessary. Lastly, sponge a weak solution of gum on the wrong side of the velvet.

Stains.

Spots on a dress are disgraceful; they should be removed the moment they are discovered.

Ink-stains on wool and cloth can be removed with oxalic acid; but to prevent it from taking out the colour, put some strong vinegar over the stain. Lemon, milk, the juice of ripe tomatoes, etc., are infallible for stains in white materials.

Should the colour of a material be accidentally destroyed by any acid, it will re-appear if the place be rubbed with ammonia. Candle-grease can be removed with eau de Cologne.

Varnish or paint stains should first be covered with butter or sweet oil, and then rubbed with turpentine. If it is an old stain, replace the turpentine by chloroform, which should of course be used with precaution.

Sherry will take out stains of claret; they must be gently rubbed with it.

Blood - stains should be soaked with petroleum, and then washed in warm water.

Fruit or any other stain should be removed by rubbing according to the grain of the material, and in no other direction.

Grease - stains are the most unsightly, more especially as they gradually increase in size. Fortunately, there are means to get rid of them. Before trying to take them out, place over them a piece of blotting-paper, iron with a hot iron, then use soap and water and ammonia. Chloroform and a mixture of alcohol and ammonia are also efficacious.

Stains can likewise be damped with ammonia and water, a piece of white paper placed over them, and ironed with a hot iron. Or they can be rubbed, on the wrong side of the stuff, with chalk, which should be left on for a day; then split a visiting-card, lay the rough side on the place, and iron lightly.

Many people prepare balls for taking out grease, so as to have them ready to hand. Make a stiff paste of fuller's-earth and vinegar, roll it into balls, and dry. To use it, grate the ball over the stain, which you must damp first. Leave it to dry, and then remove it with tepid water. Here are three more recipes for lotions and mixtures for removing stains :—

(1) Twenty - six parts of very pure spirits of turpentine, 31 parts of alcohol at 40°, and 31 parts of sulphuric ether. Cork the bottle, and shake well to mix the ingredients. In using the mixture, spread your material over a cloth thickly folded; damp the stain with the liquid, and rub

lightly with a soft rag.   If it is an old stain,
warm the place first.

(2) Mix equal parts of ammonia, ether,
and alcohol.   Wet the stain with a sponge,
then put a piece of blotting-paper over it,
damp it with the mixture, and rub the place.
In an instant it is absorbed, and dispersed
by the sponge and the paper.

(3) Here is a recipe which no stain will
resist:—Pour two quarts of clean spring-
water into a large bottle, add a piece of
white amber about the size of a walnut, a
piece of potash the size of a hazel-nut, and
two lemons cut into slices.   Let it stand
twenty-four hours.   Strain, and keep it in
well-corked bottles.   Damp the stain with
it, and rub the place with fresh water immediately afterwards.

Little Hints on Various Matters of Dress.

Faded ribbons can be cleaned in a cold
lather; they should be rinsed, shaken, and

spread upon the ironing-board, covered with muslin, and ironed while damp.

Long crape veils falling from the back of the bonnet, and crape trimming on the dresses worn in mourning, are often more spoilt by the ignorance of the lady's-maid than by the rain. Crape should be quickly dried by being spread out, but never put near the fire. If it is stained with mud, wash it in cold water, and dry it without exposing it to the sun, the air, or the fire. If the crape has become limp, put it round a wooden roller, damping it throughout with brandy. Milk may also be used to damp it, and will restore the colour, but it should be carefully sponged afterwards. The black thread stockings which are worn in mourning during summer are washed as follows :—You must not use soap, but a sort of lather made with bran (about a teacupful), shaken about in tepid water in a muslin bag. Wash your stockings in this; when you take them out of the water, roll them up in a clean cloth, wringing them out well, and dry them by a quick fire, not in the open air.

By this process the stockings will keep a good black instead of turning brown. If this precaution has been neglected, and they have turned rusty, the colour can be restored by boiling them in a quart of water, to which have been added some shavings of logwood.

A felt hat may be drenched without being spoilt, but do not let it dry without brushing it. Unpick the trimming at once, begin to brush round the edge, and continue in the same way till you come to the middle of the crown, then place it on a block, and let it dry before putting it away. It will be as good as new. Nothing is better for preserving white dresses than wrapping them up in blue paper. Although you should be careful not to crush the trimmings, the garments should be so covered as to entirely exclude the air. They should then be hung up in the wardrobe. White silk dresses should have a second covering of linen. The bodices should be put separately in boxes of their own. The trains should be left hanging their full length.

To clean the collars of garments, dissolve one part salt in four parts alcohol, put it on with a sponge, and rub well.

Cloth, serge, and felt hats may be cleaned with a short hard brush dipped in spirits of ammonia. Brush till the grease-spots have disappeared.

APPENDIX.

Stings of Insects.

COUNTRY life has one great drawback : we refer to the unbearable stings of mosquitoes or gnats. If you are stung, run into the garden for a leek or an onion, and rub the place with it. This is, no doubt, a remedy as heroic as it is excellent.

The leaves of scented verbena keep off unpleasant insects; and washing with vinegar and water or syringa-flower-water preserves the skin against their onslaughts. Honey-and-water allays the irritation produced by them; use a teaspoonful of honey in a quart of boiling water, putting it on the place while the liquid is tepid.

Flour applied on the sting takes away redness, itching, and swelling. A good and easy remedy can be made by covering it with a little soap and water, letting the lather dry on the skin.

Lastly, a small quantity of menthol mixed with alcohol is excellent as a lotion for the painful stings of wasps, bees, gnats, and nettles.

Many people use little sticks of butter of cocoa as a cosmetic. If a little cocaine (2 per cent.) be added to it, and the sting rubbed with the stick, it will procure immediate relief, and the irritation will diminish at once.

If a bee has mistaken red lips for a rose or a white brow for a lily, and if you have nothing better at hand to cure the wound inflicted by the busy insect beloved of Virgil, rub the sting with a bunch of parsley for several minutes. Chloroform is also very useful for mosquito bites; it diminishes the swelling, the irritation, and the pain which they cause. Ammonia is equally good for these little bites. Before applying it, remove the sting which the insect may have left in, and then dab the place with the alkali.

Migraine and Neuralgia.

External applications of oil of peppermint are much recommended for the terrible pain of neuralgia. The simple remedy recommended by a country doctor of poultices of black night-shade (plant and berries) is rapid and permanent in its effects. The same doctor ordered a spoonful of common salt to be taken directly a patient showed the first symptoms of migraine, and the indisposition disappeared in half an hour : a harsh remedy, certainly, but, to save hours of suffering, worth trying.

It is stated that the Queen, who was very subject to bad headaches when she was middle-aged, used to have her temples lightly stroked with a camel's-hair pencil, which cured her in a quarter of an hour.

A negress has been known to relieve her mistress from the same distressing complaint by applying slices of lemon to her temples, and pressing her head firmly.

Inflammations.

Poultices of cooked apples are good for styes and inflammation of the eyelids. Crushed leaves of bindweed applied to styes are also very efficacious.

Insomnia.

Pillows stuffed with camel's-hair, and covered with the skin of the same animal, are useful against insomnia.

Hops have the same properties, and so have onions. Sleep on a mattress of the former, and inhale the latter.

Hay-Fever.

This indisposition concerns us, for it makes the sufferer look ugly and almost ridiculous. Its symptoms are well known: a red and swollen nose, eyes full of tears, a smothered voice, constant sneezing, etc. etc. No beauty can withstand it.

It should therefore be struggled against from the beginning. Aromatic vinegar is much used as a remedy in England; a little is poured into the hand, and is inhaled up the nostrils till it is quite evaporated.

Some doctors recommend inhaling salt water several times a day, others ammonia (the bottle containing it being held to the nostrils for a minute at a time, and then withdrawn); and a little camphorated powder used like snuff sometimes has good results.

FINIS.

KINDNESS TO WOMEN.

Nothing can be more kind than to give you a Perfect Complexion.

THIS I CAN, WILL, AND DO ACCOMPLISH BY USING

ANNA RUPPERT'S
CELEBRATED SKIN TONIC.

No further use of laudation. SKIN TONIC is a cure ; and, as represented, needs no more extensive advertising. Everybody knows what it means. Cleanses, invigorates, and tones the muscles. Cures acne, eczema, &c.—in fact, all discolourations and eruptions. Is not a cosmetic, but an external medicine.

Price, per bottle, 10s. 6d. ; *three Bottles (usually required),* 25s.

ANNA RUPPERT'S valuable **"Book of Beauty"** sent free for 2d. postage.

NEW AMERICAN CORSET (already popular in England), long-waisted, ease, and grace; price, from 12s. 6d.

Artistic Manicuring. Hands Beautified, 4s. 6d. Full Line of Manicuring Instruments, &c.

CHIROPODY, REASONABLE RATES.

All Information cheerfully given Free of Charge. All Matters Confidential. Call or Address—

ANNA RUPPERT, 89, Regent Street, London, W.

Also at 8, King Street, MANCHESTER ; 124, Western Road, BRIGHTON ; 7, Cherry Street, BIRMINGHAM ; 3A, Shandwick Place, EDINBURGH ; 17, Rue de la Paix, PARIS ; BARCELONA ; SYDNEY, &c.

367

TASTELESS.—PEARL COATED.
BEST FAMILY MEDICINE.

WATSON'S COMPOUND CASTOR OIL PILLS

For Both Sexes, all Ages, Children and Adults.

FIFTY YEARS' EXPERIENCE has emphatically proved these Pills to be a certain preserver of health, a safe and speedy cure for INDIGESTION, BILIOUSNESS, HEADACHE, PILES, DIZZINESS, WIND, and DISORDERED LIVER.

Sole Proprietor: S. WAND, Leicester.

Retail by Medicine Vendors throughout the World. Price 7½d., 1s. 1½d., and 2s. 9d. per box.

Ask for WATSON'S COMPOUND CASTOR OIL PILLS, and see you get them.

Every Month, price 4d. ; or by post, 5½d.

Cassell's Time Tables
AND
Through-Route Glance-Guide.

A SUBSCRIBER writes :—*"I always buy your 'Time Tables,' and although I travel almost every day, have never yet found any mistake in it, and I consider it more useful and at the same time more simple than any other book of the kind."*

** CASSELL'S TIME TABLES may be obtained of all Booksellers and Newsagents, and at the Railway Bookstalls and Receiving Houses throughout the Kingdom.

JEWSBURY & BROWN'S

Oriental
WHITE, SOUND TEETH. HEALTHY GUMS TO OLD AGE.

Tooth
Paste

CAUTION. — The only genuine is JEWSBURY & BROWN'S.

Pots 1/6 and 2/6. All Chemists. 60 YEARS IN USE.

373

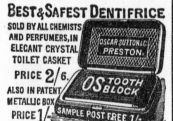

THE FOLDING DRESSING GLASS.

One of the most perfect Toilette Glasses of the day, showing seven different views of a Head Dress, and when not opened its appearance is that of an Ordinary Dressing Glass. It affords ample accommodation for Toilette Articles, Jewellery, &c. &c., all of which are secured automatically in the act of closing by Patent Spring Locks. The drawing shows one half open, and the other closed.

The prices are from £5 to £10, according to size and details.

Fuller particulars post free on application.

Dressing Tables with the Folding Glass combined, from £7 to £17 each.

TRAPNELL & GANE,
COMPLETE HOUSE FURNISHERS.

Head Establishment and Manufactories:
38a, 39, and 40, COLLEGE GREEN, BRISTOL.

Branches:
38 & 45, Queen Street, Cardiff; 161 & 162, Commercial Street, Newport, Mon.

ESTABLISHED 70 YEARS.

All Articles purchased at either of these Establishments are delivered, Carriage Paid, to any Railway Station in the Kingdom.

Illustrated Furnishing Guide, 1,000 Engravings, Post Free.

GODFREY'S EXTRACT OF ELDER FLOWERS

Has long been known for its surprising effect in softening, improving, and preserving the Skin, and in rendering the COMPLEXION clear and beautiful.

It removes Tan, Sunburn, Redness. It cures Pimples, Humours, Eruptions.

As a TOILET REQUISITE, it is unsurpassed.

In the Nursery it is indispensable, giving immediate relief to Infants bitten by Insects. Gentlemen will find it delightfully soothing after Shaving.

AS a family lotion, to use on all occasions, Godfrey's Extract of Elder Flowers will be found beyond all praise, and needs only a trial to be approved. Its agreeable perfume, its pleasing and beneficial effects in rendering the complexion delicately clear and beautiful, in softening the skin, cleansing its pores, and freeing it from all pimples and eruptions, in improving its colour, and conferring a transcendent transparency and bloom, and rendering it altogether unexceptionable, are so prompt and decided that it must ultimately supersede the use of all other preparations. Indeed, it only requires a comparison to show, in the strongest light, its amazing superiority.

To children it is singularly beneficial, and perfectly innoxious, even to the youngest infant. It will cleanse the pores of the skin, clear off dandruff much better than combs, will quickly relieve all those inflammatory affections of the face, neck, and ears, occasioned by teething, chafing, &c., and give an appearance of cleanliness and health truly surprising—must be seen to be believed ; and will indisputably show that it is alike the *ne plus ultra* of the nursery and of the toilette.

GODFREY'S EXTRACT OF ELDER FLOWERS, SOLD EVERYWHERE, PRICE 2/9